FITZROVIA

by Nick Bailey

FITZROVIA

by Nick Bailey

HISTORICAL PUBLICATIONS
in association with
CAMDEN HISTORY SOCIETY

ISBN 0 9503656 2 9

First published 1981
Printed in Great Britain by
Eyre and Spottiswoode, at
The Grosvenor Press.
Typeset by Body Copy.

Published by
Historical Publications Ltd
54 Station Road
New Barnet, Herts.
in association with the Camden History Society.

Acknowledgements

I am very grateful to' the staff of Camden Libraries at St Pancras, Holborn and Swiss Cottage for obtaining the often obscure and out-of-print volumes during my research. In particular I would like to thank Malcolm Holmes and his staff at the Local History Library at Swiss Cottage for their help. I have also received valuable assistance at the libraries of the Polytechnic of Central London and those at County Hall. John Richardson deserves special thanks for encouraging and supporting this work from the beginning.

Finally I would like to thank all those residents who, often unwittingly, have suggested leads and areas for further research. Any omissions are entirely my responsibility.

The Illustrations

The illustrations in this book are reproduced with the kind permission of:

London Borough of Camden: *3, 4, 6, 7, 8, 9, 10, 13, 14, 15, 16, 17, 19, 21, 24, 26, 32, 33, 35, 39, 40, 42, 44*
Greater London Council: *20, 36, 41*
The Well Woman Centre, Whitfield Street: *43*
The Guildhall Library: *5, 30*
Messrs Heal and Son Ltd: *37*
National Portrait Gallery: *12, 18, 22, 23*
Illustrations *11, 25, 27, 28, 31, 34, 38, 45* are the property of the author

Cover illustration: The carton-Pierre ornament workshop of George Jackson & Sons Ltd, 49 Rathbone Place, 1908.

Reproduced with the kind permission of the Royal Institute of British Architects

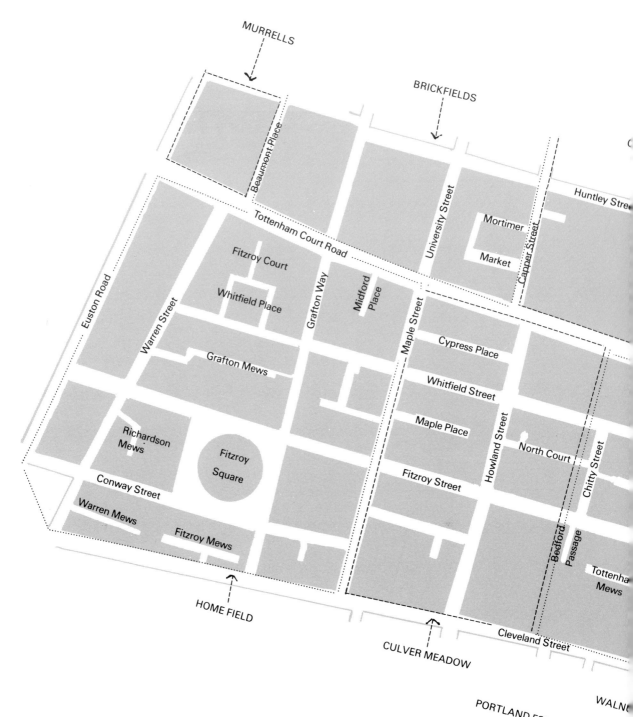

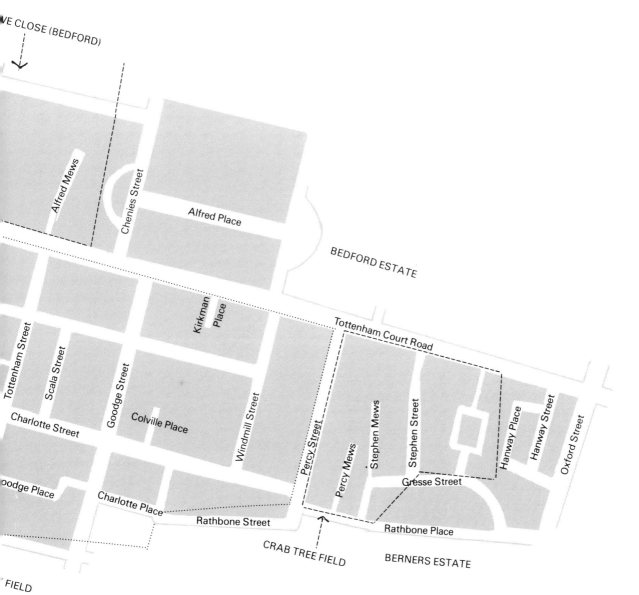

WE CLOSE (BEDFORD)

Alfred Mews

Chenies Street

Alfred Place

BEDFORD ESTATE

Kirkman Place

Tottenham Court Road

Tottenham Street

Scala Street

Goodge Street

Colville Place

Windmill Street

Percy Street

Percy Mews

Stephen Mews

Stephen Street

Hanway Place

Hanway Street

Oxford Street

Charlotte Street

oodge Place

Charlotte Place

Rathbone Street

Gresse Street

Rathbone Place

CRAB TREE FIELD

BERNERS ESTATE

FIELD

FITZROVIA

Based upon the Ordnance Survey
with the permission of
The Controller of Her Majesty's Stationery Office,
Crown Copyright Reserved

Introduction

Fitzrovia is a wedge of central London stretching north from Oxford Street and defined by the ancient boundaries of the Bedford Estate in the east and Portland Estate in the west. Over the last two hundred years it has developed a character all of its own — cosmopolitan but fundamentally tawdry, cheap and Bohemian — resulting partly from its pattern of Georgian streets and buildings and partly from the arts, crafts and trades that have always been pursued here. While attracting colonies of artists, writers and poets over the years, its streets have rarely provided fashionable addresses for the famous; it has more often provided a refuge for the eccentric and impecunious. What is perhaps most surprising is that the area never received a commonly accepted name until the 1940s when it flowered briefly as the haunt of artists and writers who congregated in the Fitzroy Tavern and surrounding pubs. Before then it was referred to as Fitzroy Square — the social apex of the area which itself fell on hard times — or the less attractive, North Soho. E. B. Chancellor, the only author of a book specifically on the area, was reduced to calling it 'London's Old Latin Quarter'.

The main conclusion seems to be that most artists and writers saw Fitzrovia merely as a convenient place to live or work; there are very few external views or written descriptions, except in reminiscences or biographies. One example of the latter by Richard Buckle in his book, *Adventures of a Ballet Critic*, sums up the character of the area in a paragraph:

'Considering what a mean and monotonous thoroughfare it is, Charlotte Street is surprisingly charged — for me at any rate — with history and significance. Like an adventuress, it keeps changing its name: Originating humbly, though on a ducal estate, in the Euston Road, then making a surprisingly brilliant march into the Duke's family and becoming one side of Fitzroy Square; soon widowed, it becomes artistic but retains its noble surname down two blocks of Fitzroy Street, where so many studios are; next, crossing Howland Street, it enters the domain of the Duke of Bedford, but marries the foreign chef and becomes Charlotte Street, famed for its exotic restaurants; then with a right-left swerve — a serious operation which leaves it with a permanent kink — it enters on a dubious old age in Rathbone Place, and expires as it began, in trade, in Oxford Street.'

Thus although Fitzrovia had and still has undoubted character, this has never coalesced into a single image which sticks in the mind. It has never been dominated by a single trade or activity like Covent Garden, achieved the social status of Chelsea or been able to erect the necessary social defences like the Bedford Estate in Bloomsbury. For perhaps twenty or thirty years from the end of the 18th century Fitzrovia achieved the social objectives of its builders, but the desire for quick returns meant that the houses were soon leased off to a vast array of service industries and insecure tenancies. Its immediate accessibility to at least three major highways and the coming of the railways to Euston in the 1830s further reinforced this trend.

Throughout its history Fitzrovia in most senses has been marginal, on the fringe of things and thus has tended to attract those on the fringes of society — the struggling artist, the self-employed cobbler, mason or woodworker and successive waves of immigrant groups, seeking cheap lodgings and employment in the many service trades of London.

How can Fitzrovia be called marginal when it so obviously lies in the heart of the West End? The explanation for this must lie in the way the area was developed — mainly by piecemeal speculation over many years — and the resulting medley of different ownerships, tenancies and leaseholders. While in the 18th century the Southampton Estate made a grand gesture at a comprehensive development around Fitzroy Square, it soon lost interest in retaining ownership as the character of the area had already changed by the time leases began to fall in. Thus the fabric of buildings was saved at least until the Second World War by the complex mosaic of ownership. Because the demand for office space was negligible outside the City in 19th century London, the Georgian houses, originally built to attract gentlemen and their families, rapidly became sub-divided both vertically and horizontally into a complex warren of rooms to let, workrooms for craftsmen and

2. A section of a c1800 map of St Pancras

artists' studios, all at relatively low rents.

This process soon became self-sustaining since because ownership was fragmented redevelopment on any scale before the days of compulsory purchase, was out of the question. At the same time, the lack of maintenance to buildings and the proximity of often noxious and noisy trades next to residential rooms and houses tended to keep rents relatively low. It was only as a result of heavy bombing and the relative decline of small service trades throughout London, that this relationship between buildings and the uses inside them was broken. As a result, redevelopment for offices in the worst hit areas — aided and abetted by the planning system — followed in the 1950s and '60s.

Nonetheless, the flavour of the area as it must have been can still be experienced in some parts of Fitzrovia. Given the ravages of Hitler and the property developers soon after, and changing social and economic patterns which have meant the gradual exodus of residents and skilled jobs from central and inner areas, some streets remain remarkably unscathed. It is still quite common, for example, to find well preserved Georgian houses with a shop inserted on the ground floor, a tailor on the first, a designer on the second and a flat on the top floor, a few yards from the Post Office Tower or an international advertising agency.

Since about 1970 there has been something of a resurgence of local feeling in the area as local residents began to realise that something had to be done quickly if what remained of the character of the area was to be saved. This led to the formation of a number of local groups and tenants' associations and in 1974, the setting up of the Fitzrovia Neighbourhood Association. While some groups were concerned with preserving the architecture of the area and improving the environment as a place to live and work, others were concerned with the struggle for better housing conditions and improved social amenities. As a result, the FNA began to pressure Camden Council on all these fronts and today the area is blessed with two conservation areas, a town scheme, two housing action areas and a concern in at least some quarters of the council that more should be done to restore the balance of housing and small workshops, in preference to further office development.

This publication will not dwell on the struggles that have taken place to conserve the existing fabric and to improve living conditions in the area; this could amply fill a book in itself. Its main purpose is to record, however briefly, something of what survives in written records of the lives of those who have lived and worked in the area. This it is hoped will stimulate the reader to investigate more closely the streets of Fitzrovia and the heritage they contain and perhaps finally to provide the parameters for a much more exhaustive and well-considered study of the area, which is long overdue.

Something should be said about the boundaries chosen for this guide. Fitzrovia, at its greatest extent, is normally assumed to extend from Great Portland Street in the west to Gower Street in the east, and from Euston Road to Oxford Street. While these last two boundaries have been kept to, the east-west boundaries have been changed partly for reasons of space. It was also felt that Cleveland Street was more appropriate as a western boundary in this case since this marks the boundary between Camden and Westminster, St Pancras and St Marylebone and the Southampton and Portland Estates. The inclusion of the area west of Cleveland Street would therefore have involved the investigation of a different history of land-holding and development for which space did not allow. On the east side all lands have been included which were not part of the Bedford Estate from an early date. Thus throughout the emphasis has been on land originally held by the Tottenhall Manor of St Pancras and subsequently owned by the Southampton Estate and other independent owners — this in itself is an indication of the importance of land-ownership in determining the future development and history of an area.

3. *Tottenhall Manor House from a 1743 painting*

The Development of Fitzrovia

London's Westward Expansion

In the past 300 years London has expanded in defiance of any restraints — legal or physical — put in its path. The motive has usually been speculative: either building along main roads or around villages and hamlets or, as in later years, the development of planned estates by aristocratic landowners on the fringes of the city. The streets of Fitzrovia resulted from both these trends, reflecting both the work of jobbing builders who just wanted to make a living, as well as the grand scheme by Lord Southampton, who wanted to make his mark on Society.

Up until the middle of the 17th century London remained an enclosed medieval city, founded on a Roman grid plan and circumscribed by an ancient city wall. Within a matter of decades in the middle of the 17th century the capital was launched on its way to becoming the 'Great Wen' of the 19th century. The turning point came after the Civil War and the period of prosperity after the restoration of Charles II in 1660. It was the Great Plague and ensuing Great Fire which enabled these pressures to be released.

As in most cases of fire, pestilence and war, the City fathers had rebuilt the capital with new materials and to new building standards (but on the old road pattern, thereby rejecting Wren's classical and comprehensive plan), expecting London within the walls to regain its former dominance and prosperity. This was not to be. During the conflagration 80,000 citizens had fled the flames for the outlying villages and by 1672 a quarter had still not returned. New houses also remained unoccupied. What had happened was that many of the merchants and traders who had been forced to flee the City were finding new prosperity, more space and lower rents outside the City's jurisdiction in areas such as the Strand, Holborn and the new development around Covent Garden.

To the west of the City development was gradual and largely uncontrolled, fanning out from High Holborn, the Strand, Covent Garden and the ancient village of St Giles-in-the-Fields. Much of this was shoddy and piecemeal. Houses or short terraces were hastily thrown up in open fields and some of the larger houses were converted to tenements or workshops, much to the annoyance of the authorities. Some of the larger landowners began to realise the potential of larger, planned and more prestigious developments.

The Russell family had already shown the advantages, financial and otherwise, of good quality design when, with the services of Inigo Jones, Covent Garden had been laid out as London's first piazza. Because of continuing royal favour and a fortuitous marriage, a generation later the same family was in a particularly strong position to begin the development of the manor of Bloomsbury. In 1669 William Russell, second son of the fifth Earl of Bedford, married Rachel Lady Vaughan, daughter and co-heir of Thomas Wriothesley, fourth and last Earl of Southampton. While William Russell was given on his marriage the benefit of the family estates in Covent Garden and Woburn, his wife had inherited on the death of her father (and after drawing lots with her sister) the manor of Bloomsbury. On this land the fourth Earl of Southampton had already constructed Southampton House and laid out the beginnings of what is now Bloomsbury Square. The remainder of the manor was then being let out to tenant farmers or as copyhold land.

By the beginning of the 18th century building had continued at such a pace that houses now extended without a break from the City of London to the City of Westminster particularly along the Strand. Just to the north development extended the length of High Holborn, through the village of St Giles, around the church and along Tyburn Road or Oxford Street. Tottenham Court Road stretched north through open fields to Tottenham Court itself and onwards to Hampstead. Great Russell Street began as a drive in front of Southampton House and Montagu House (later the site of the British Museum) but ended as a track where it met Tottenham Court Road.

On the west side of Tottenham Court Road and its eastern fringes development took place in a very different manner to the neighbouring Bedford Estate. The area we now know as Fitzrovia was fragmented in ownership and consequently was developed in a far more shortsighted and speculative approach. Since landowners sold off plots to the highest bidder with few legal or financial safeguards, the small-time builders that sought quick returns but at a high risk have left their mark on the arca today.

The Parish of St Pancras, the Manor of Tottenhall

The wedge of land now called Fitzrovia is a part of the ancient parish of St Pancras which stretched from Oxford Street to Highgate. The map on pages 6 & 7 shows the western and eastern boundaries of the Fitzrovia portion and it will be seen that large secular estates as well as parishes surrounded it.

At the time of Domesday Book St Pancras was in the ownership of the Canons of St Paul's Cathedral, although leases on parts of the holding changed hands with considerable ease and frequency. The church seems rarely able to master the secular responsibilities of property ownership and the Canons of St Paul's were no exception. They were content to remain as absentee landlords, collecting the steadily increasing rental income of the land as an agricultural holding.

Domesday Book records that St Pancras was divided into four manors: Fitzrovia fell within Tottenhall which stretched right up to Kenwood. The manor house, Tottenham Court, stood between Tolmers Square and Euston Road.

At the outbreak of the Civil War the manor was expropriated by Parliament and sold to a Londoner, Ralph Harrison, for the considerable sum of £3,318. With the restoration of Charles II, it was repossessed by the Crown and in 1667 was given by the King to Henry Benet, Earl of Arlington, Principal Secretary of State, 'in consideration of his many and great services'. The Arlingtons' country seat was at Euston Hall in Suffolk. In 1672 the Earl's daughter, Isabella, married Henry Fitzroy, one of Charles II's many illegitimate children by Barbara Villiers, Duchess of Cleveland. On their marriage, Henry was created Earl of Euston and three years later first Duke of Grafton.

For the next two generations of the Fitzroy family the estates in Tottenhall and Euston, Suffolk, were held as one, but on the death of the second Duke of Grafton in 1757, his grandson Augustus Henry became the third Duke of Grafton and inherited the Euston estate. His younger brother, Charles Fitzroy, was left the lease of Tottenhall manor and to reflect his improved station in life was made first Baron Southampton in 1780.

There has always been a degree of confusion about the Southampton title which at different times has been connected with both the Russell and Fitzroy families. The Southampton peerage was first held by the Wriothesley family and, as has been seen, on the death of the fourth and last Earl, the Bloomsbury estate was inherited by his daughter Rachel on her marriage. The title was revived only in 1780 when Charles Fitzroy assumed the title Baron Southampton. There was therefore no blood relationship between the Fitzroys and Wriothesleys or Russells.

In 1757 Charles Fitzroy was well placed to reap the benefits of the Tottenhall estate left to him by his grandfather. All that stood in his way was the need to obtain the freehold of the manor from the Canons of St Paul's so that building plots could be sold off for development. This was secured with no great difficulty in 1768 by Act of Parliament, as a writer in the *Morning Chronicle* in 1837 recalled:

'In the year 1768, the Duke of Grafton was Prime Minister. His brother, Mr Fitzroy, was lessee of the manor and lordship of Tottenhall, the property of the Dean and Chapter of St Paul's London. Dr Richard Brown, the then prebendary of the stall of Tottenhall, having pocketed the emolument attending the renewal of the lease, and there being little chance of any further advantages to him from the estate, readily listened to a proposal of Mr Fitzroy for the purchase of the estate. The thing was agreed, and the Duke of Grafton, with his great standing majority, quickly passed an Act of Parliament, in March 1768, diverting the estate, with all its rights, privileges, and emoluments from the prebend, and conveying the fee-simple entire, and without reserve, to Mr Charles Fitzroy and his heirs for ever. The Act states it to be with the consent of Richard, Lord Bishop of London, and the privity of the Dean and Chapter of St Paul's.'

For this transaction the church was to receive

the relatively small sum of £300 a year; a little over six times the annual rental (£46) that was then being charged for the leasehold. The *Morning Chronicle* then went on to criticise the 'noble conservators of the poor man's church' for handing over such a potentially valuable estate and calculated that by 1837 the Southampton family had already made £1.5m from the development of the estate. In mitigation of this transaction, the *Survey of London* (Vol. XXI) argues that the Fitzroys really only obtained the development rights to about 255 acres of the demesne lands of the manor, since most of the occupiers of customary or copyhold land had enfranchised themselves by paying quit rents over a great many years. Whatever the conclusions about the deal, the Fitzroys managed to purchase the freehold on distinctly generous terms, which bore little relation to the potential value of the estate after development.

The New Road

This astute move by the Fitzroys cannot have gone unnoticed even by the generally low ethical standards of the eighteenth century. Clearly they felt themselves sufficiently well placed both in Parliament and the royal court to fend off any opposition. In fact, gaining the freehold of the manor by Act of Parliament was part of a longer term strategy instituted a decade earlier when the second Duke of Grafton became a keen supporter of the New Road. This was a new turnpike road to be built from Paddington to Islington, now called the Marylebone, Euston and Pentonville Roads, under an Act of Parliament approved in 1756.

This Act had been vigorously opposed by the Duke of Bedford on the grounds that it would lead to development which would obstruct his view of the Hampstead and Highgate hills from Bedford House and would devalue his agricultural lands to the south. The Duke of Grafton took the opposite view and saw immediately the advantages the New Road would bring in opening up his family's estate, particularly around Tottenham Court. Press reports of the time record how on its completion, the Duke of Grafton led an unruly procession, on a Sunday, down the New Road, 'accompanied by a great company as little sensible of religion as himself'.

Tottenham Court and the Manor House

The manor house at Tottenham Court had long been a landmark in the area and while remaining the centre of a large agricultural holding was also becoming a place of resort for Londoners who walked across the fields to it at weekends and holidays.

Early records are sparse and on occasions contradictory but it is known that it stood from Tudor times, if not before, between the now demolished Tolmers Square and the Euston Road. The house is first recorded in a plan and survey by William Necton in 1591, when the manor was held by the Crown and occupied by Daniel Clarke, Master Cook to Elizabeth I. He calls it 'a very slender building of timber and brick' which 'hath been of a larger building than now is. For some little parte hath been pulled down of late to amend some parte of the houses now standing'. A later survey in 1649 found the house standing in 1½ acres of grounds surrounded by a moat. A gatehouse led into a courtyard and the hall was divided into a wainscotted parlour at one end and a kitchen, larder and cellar at the other. A staircase led up to a great chamber with an inner room, seven other rooms and a pair of back stairs.

The Heal Collection contains a water colour drawing by W. Burden in 1801, which is described as a copy of a painting of the house in 1743. This shows a traditional manor house which may well have had an additional wing on the right, as hinted at by Necton's description. While the Elizabethan part of the house was probably demolished in the mid 18th century, the older building seen on the left survived till 1808. This was known as King John's Palace, but there is no known historical connection with that king.

According to Rocque's map of 1746, the manor house was surrounded by gardens and orchards and a pond is shown approximately on the site of the former Tolmers Square (in 1802 a reservoir was built here by the New River Company). A turnpike is shown at the southern end of Hampstead Road close by the Adam and Eve public house, also surrounded by gardens. On land where the present Warren Street tube station stands further farm buildings with courtyards are shown. Hogarth's painting the *March of the*

Guards to Finchley (1749), clearly shows the Adam and Eve and the King's Head with an uninterrupted vista of the northern heights in the background.

In 1979 an excavation of the site before redevelopment revealed little more than a few foundation walls and what was most likely the cesspit of the manor house.

Tottenham Court Fair

Throughout the 17th and 18th centuries Tottenham Court became particularly popular with the clerks and craftsmen of the City, who at weekends and public holidays, walked across the fields to sample the delights of the Adam and Eve, which then was known for the springs in its garden, and the King's Head. By all accounts the area soon developed a reputation for riotous behaviour and loose morals. The Heal Collection contains the lines by an unknown 17th century playwright:

'Y'are welcome Gentlemen to Tot'nam Court,
Where you (perhaps) expect some lusty sport,
Such as rude custom doth beget in hay,
When straggling numbers court that jovial day,
With early riot. No such thing must be,
The subject of our easie comedie.'

By the beginning of the 18th century, Tottenham Court became host to an annual fair of that name, although later it was called Gooseberry Fair, and in its heyday provided a major source of amusement and entertainment for Londoners. Stalls, theatrical booths, displays of boxing and physical prowess were all common, and if the surviving records of the authorities are to be believed, gambling, drunken brawls and frequent acts of indecency. During the fair of 1785 Lunardi, one of the first hot-air balloonists, descended into Tottenham Court Road after having just taken off from Moorfields, and was mobbed by a crowd.

By 1808, when the area was almost entirely built up apart from the gardens of the Adam and Eve, the authorities were finally able to suppress the fair, with the assistance of the Trustees of the New Road, when the obstruction of the highway by stall-holders became intolerable.

Both pubs were eventually demolished in road widening schemes; the King's Head in 1906, the Adam and Eve in the 1960s to make way for the Euston Centre.

4. *King John's Palace*

Meadow Land to Slum

Although the Fitzroys had obtained the freehold of the manor, this did not nullify leases and rights held under the ancient system of law by which holders of copyhold or customary leasehold had almost the same rights as outright owners. Much of the land to the west of Tottenham Court Road and parts on the east side were held in this way. This meant that the development of these particular holdings was largely under the control of 'tenants', who, to complicate matters for the historian, could also sell their rights to the land *as though* they were freeholders. In fact only two parts of the area under consideration fell within the 'demesne' lands of the manor, and it was only here that the Fitzroys had complete control over the way the land was developed. The most important of these was Home Field, the area which became Fitzroy Square and surrounding streets. The other was a thin strip of land to the south of the New Road, running from Tottenham Court Road to the new St Pancras Church, and on this houses along Euston Road and Euston Square were eventually constructed.

The system of urban development was complex in the eighteenth century, especially as in certain circumstances those not in sole possession of the freehold had a right to sell building leases. This system enabled landowners to develop their land at no financial risk to themselves but if all went well, they received a gradually increasing income from ground rent and potentially a large financial gain when the leases expired. The land to be developed would be divided into building plots and leased to an intermediary, usually a builder or other craftsman, for a period of up to 99 years at a relatively low ground rent. The builder then constructed the houses at his own expense, often to standards determined by the landowner, and then had the problem of selling leases on the properties sufficient to cover his costs and to provide a reasonable living. At the end of the 99 years the buildings reverted to the ground landlord who could then renew the leases for a greatly increased rent, sell the buildings and land individually to the occupiers or put them on the open market.

Nineteenth century commentators such as Charles Booth often remarked on the perversity of this speculative system of development which encouraged leaseholders and their tenants to neglect the essential maintenance of property which was soon to revert to the ground landlord. This also meant that landowners often sold out just before the leases were due to expire and in this way many of the smaller estates were auctioned off when the majority of leases fell in. In exceptional cases, landlords like the Duke of Bedford were able to maintain the quality of estates by threatening negligent tenants with legal action if they did not maintain their property, and by preventing the infiltration of multi-occupation and commercial users that might lower the tone of the area.

The Southampton Estate soon found it impossible to maintain the social standing of its property. This was because apart from small enclaves like Fitzroy and Bedford Squares, the gentry had already moved westwards, and it is quite likely that many leaseholders were sub-letting their houses soon after they were completed. By the middle of the 19th century large parts of Fitzrovia were densely occupied by the poor and immigrant families, while the ground floors were converted to shops and workrooms. By Victorian standards the area had been reduced to a slum. Given this gradual decline, the Fitzroys could do little but sell off what must have become a considerable embarrassment to them and concentrate on their Suffolk Estate.

For an investigation of the development of Fitzrovia one of the best places to start is Cassell's map of London of 1720. This clearly shows that at that date there were no buildings north of Oxford Street on either side of Tottenham Court Road. Only tracks and field boundaries are marked which relate more or less to roads and areas of development which figure later in the century.

Within the next 25 years a considerable flurry of development must have taken place, since on Rocque's map of 1746 buildings are then shown up as far as Percy Street and across to Rathbone Place. Further sporadic development can also be seen on the west side of Tottenham Court Road up to Windmill Street and beyond. The beginnings of the Cavendish/Holles (Portland) Estate are appearing around Cavendish Square and Mortimer Street and the development of the

Berners Estate around Newman Street was well under way.

The development of Fitzrovia took place in fits and starts. In the years of depression terraces remained uncompleted and new streets petered out into the open fields. Brickfields and shallow ponds littered the area. When the economy boomed, a feverish spate of building activity would take place with whole streets being laid out and constructed in a matter of months. The 1720s and '30s, 1760s and 1790s all witnessed large extensions to the area.

Fitzrovia falls neatly into a series of fields which were developed one by one as their owners felt the time was right. *(See Illustration pp 6 & 7)*. The small field nearest Oxford Street was the first to be transformed, then followed Crab Tree and Walnut Tree Fields a little further north, the Bedford Estate tried its hand at Culver Meadow and finally the Fitzroys attempted to meet the highest standards on Home Field. With hindsight the process appears gradual and logical but in reality it was haphazard in the extreme. While owners tended to go for good quality housing to ensure their land retained its value, it was the many jobbing builders who had to construct and let the houses in the face of market forces.

The Hanway and Rathbone Developments

The southern boundary of Tottenhall manor did not quite reach as far as Oxford Street but left a small meadow lying mainly in St Marylebone. In 1595 this was sold by Lord Mountjoy to Edward Kyngeston, a brickmaker of St Martins-in-the-Fields, and was described as extending 2½ acres, partly in St Marylebone and partly in St Pancras, and was let at the time to Nicholas Holden. It had formerly been owned by the Hospital of St Giles, but by the early 18th century was in the possession of the Hanway family. Hanway Street and Petty's Court (now Hanway Place), according to contemporary maps, must have been built between 1720 and the mid 1740s. Thomas Hanway was a commissioner for the Royal Navy and Jonas Hanway, after travelling in the Middle East as a merchant took up good causes in the capital. In 1756 he founded the Marine Society to supply trained sailors to the navy and in 1758 was made a governor of the Foundling Hospital.

Until 1900 the parish and manorial boundary ran down the centre of what is now Rathbone Street; this was first called Glanville Street and later Upper Rathbone Place. Very little is known about this land which seems to have included Rathbone Place, Evelyn Yard and Rathbone Street — a long, thin strip of land which nowhere exceeds about 50 yards wide and was bordered by the Berners Estate. All that is known is that a Captain Thomas Rathbone owned the land in 1684 and that he must have been of some standing as he was a churchwarden the same year. His son and daughter-in-law, Dr John and Mrs Rathbone lived here in the 1720s and '30s. In 1740 land on either side of Rathbone Place belonged to William Glanville. His only child and heiress, Frances, married William Evelyn of St Clare, Kent, a descendant of John Evelyn the diarist, and it was their children that built Evelyn Yard, linking Rathbone Place and Gresse Street.

The building of Rathbone Place seems to have begun at the southern end about 1720, extending slowly northwards. Building leases were being sold in Rathbone Street in the 1760s. A precise date can be fixed on the building of one house on the corner of Rathbone Street and Percy Street — still standing and now the Marquis of Granby. This was leased by William Franks to Joseph Francis in 1765 and assigned by Edmund Pepys and Joseph Francis to Bartholomew Hammond in July 1767, by which time the building may well have been completed. Before the 1760s the west side of Charlotte Street and most of Rathbone Street were covered by what Rocque calls Merchant's Water Works. This was a windmill (hence Windmill Street), which both pumped water to the fountain in Soho Square and ground corn. There was also a rectangular pond close by, fed by a spring which was contained in a cellar of a house in Rathbone Street when the land was built on.

J. T. Smith, the biographer of the sculptor Joseph Nollekens, who for many years lived in Mortimer Street, remembers how he used to visit the windmill as a child:

'Mr Nollekens stopped at the corner of Rathbone Place, and observed that, when he was a little boy, his mother often took him to the top of

5. Percy Chapel

that street to walk by the side of a long pond, near a windmill, which then stood on the site of the chapel in Charlotte Street; and that a halfpenny was paid by every person at a hatch belonging to the miller, for the privilege of walking in his grounds.'

The chapel in Charlotte Street referred to is the Percy Chapel, built in 1765 by William Franks under a lease granted by Francis and William Goodge. This must be about the time when the windmill and pond disappeared.

Crab Tree and Walnut Tree Fields

The precise boundary between these fields is unclear. Rocque's 1769 map refers to what became Goodge Street as Crabtree Street and the boundary could have been here.

However the part of this area south of Percy Street was leased by John Dudley to John Hassell, a brewer, in 1717. Hassell also had premises, later to be Meux's brewery, on the site of the Dominion Theatre. He built houses along the Tottenham Court Road frontage of his new acquisition as far as Percy Street and also houses at the southern end of Gresse Street. His own house and two acre garden covered the rest. In 1752 his estate was sold in lots. The Hassell house and garden were purchased by Peter Gaspard Gresse. His son was John Alexander Gresse, the painter known as Jack Grease, who was appointed drawing master to the royal princesses in 1777. In 1768 Gresse laid out part of Gresse Street and Stephen Street, in partnership with his neighbour, Stephen Caesar Lemaistre, on the former site of Hassell's house and garden. Although most of Gresse Street was cleared to make way for workshops and warehouses a number of the finer houses in Stephen Street survived until the early 1970s.

Since the lease granted in 1717 by John Dudley was for a period of 111 years, this expired in 1828 and all the property reverted to John Dudley's descendants. Although in the intervening years the estate had been divided among surviving children, by 1819 it seems that at least part of the estate was held by one Elizabeth Mary Jones, who married first George Tudor M.P. for Barnstaple (hence Tudor Place) and secondly in 1861 John Vereker, 3rd Viscount Gort, who died in 1865.

Whether the Gort Estate remained in the Gort family's ownership remains unknown since, on the sale of the land to EMI Ltd who have built an office complex here, the estate papers were deposited in the GLC Records Office and they have yet to be filed or catalogued.

Crabtree Fort
One of the few occasions in history when London faced a military threat was during the Civil War. Crab Tree Field, being the nearest piece of open ground close to the junction of Oxford Street and Tottenham Court Road, was immediately identified as a suitable location for a defensive garrison.

It was in 1642 that London came out in support of Cromwell and immediately set about building a series of forts and earthworks in anticipation of an attack by royalist forces. A contemporary report records how:

'The Committee for the Militia of London have given order that Trenches and Ramparts shall be raised neere all the roads and highwaies that come to the City, as about St James, St Gyles in the Fields, beyond Islington and about St Pancras Church in the fields, and they are now busily at worke about them......'

A total of 18 miles of trenches, three yards thick and on the ditch side six yards high, linking 24 forts were constructed, just outside the limits of the built-up area. A contemporary observer, William Lithgow, in his *Surveigh of London* (1643) records a walk he made along these defences. To the north of London forts were placed just to the east of Grays Inn Road, in the garden of Southampton House on the north side of Bloomsbury Square, at the junction of Great Russell Street and Tottenham Court Road and in Crab Tree Field, just to the north of the present Hanway Place. The rampart then crossed Oxford Street to another fort near Wardour Street.

In order to complete this task as quickly as possible, the City mobilised up to 100,000 able-bodied persons and Lithgow notes how even fish-wives were marched from Billingsgate through Cheapside to Crab Tree Field, 'the goddess Bellona leading them in a martial way'. With such a fearsome army of occupation, it is not surprising that Lithgow comments on the great damage done to grazing land in the vicinity and forecasts great hardship for local farmers.

In the event the defences remained untried and the nearest the Royalists got to London was Turnham Green. In September 1647 Parliament ordered the forts to be demolished and within a matter of years most traces of them disappeared.

Walnut Tree Field
In 1717 when Dudley let Crab Tree Field, or part of it, to Hassell, he leased the remaining 16 acres of the two fields to William Beresford, again for 111 years. The boundary of this larger holding ran just to the north of Whitefield's Tabernacle, through Chitty Street (formerly North Street), along Bedford Passage, to the south of the former St Paul's Covent Garden workhouse (now the Middlesex Hospital Out-Patients' Department) and down Cleveland Street.

J. T. Smith, in his other minor masterpiece, *A Book for a Rainy Day*, remembered how in the 1760s a rope-walk and 'two magnificent rows of elms' extended north from the workhouse along the Green Lane, now Cleveland Street, as far as Farthing Pie House (now the Green Man on the Euston Road). The landscape painter, Richard Wilson was also to be seen sketching under the elms.

In 1718, however, William Beresford died and the property passed to his wife Ann, who married John Goodge, a carpenter. It was John Goodge, together with his nephews Francis and William Goodge, who developed most of the land, which remained within the family until the 19th century. Relatively little is known about John Goodge or his nephews except that he died in 1748 aged 57 and was buried alongside his wife, who died in 1741, in old St Pancras churchyard.

Even less is known about the extent of the involvement of the Goodge family in the development of the estate. John Goodge, being a carpenter, may well have worked in the Windmill Street area, for which building leases were sold on the south side in 1723-4. The street was not fully completed and occupied until about 1770. Goodge Place (originally Cumberland Street) may also have been under construction in the last decade of John Goodge's life, since it is dated by Sir John Summerson to within the decade 1740-50, according to architectural evidence.

For about thirty years after the death of John Goodge there was a period of increased building activity in St Pancras, partly in response to favourable economic circumstances and partly because London's population was increasing rapidly. Francis and William Goodge must also have been busy at this time. In 1764 they granted a building lease on the south side of Percy Street and in 1766 on the north side, possibly to William Franks. Franks had already been sold a lease on ground on the west side of Charlotte Street, where the Percy Chapel was built in 1765. A year later, the *Survey of London* records that Franks bought a lease from the Goodge brothers on a strip of land running from Charlotte Street to Whitfield Street, on which Colville Place was laid out. Franks was unable to do the work himself so a few months later sold the lease to Edmund Pepys, who financed the construction of 'a new intended court 18 feet wide to be called Colvill Court'. For this John Colvill, a carpenter, appears to have been the builder most involved. Alas, it was too much for him and he went bankrupt in 1774.

In 1767 the Goodge brothers launched their most ambitious scheme which was 'the intended new street designed to be called Goodge Street'. It was intended to be a shopping thoroughfare from the beginning and by 1770 development was well

advanced and over half the properties were occupied. Numbers 11 to 15 (now 22 to 30) were under construction in 1766, after a lease had been granted the same year to Richard Guyatt for nos. 11—14 for 62 years and to Thomas Boughton for number 15. Both men were carpenters. Designs for this part of the street were drawn up by Jacob Leroux, an architect of some importance, who about the same time had designed a Polygon at Southampton and in 1793 erected a circus of houses with the same name in Somers Town. The first occupants of Goodge Street in the 1760s included carpenters, oil men, tallow chandlers, undertakers, soap and candle makers, ironmongers, tobacconists and a silk dyer — trades associated with Fitzrovia for at least 200 years.

By the early 1770s a rapid spate of building in Crab Tree and Walnut Tree fields, particularly Goodge Street, Scala Street, Goodge Place and parts of Tottenham Street, meant that the land as far as Chitty Street was almost completely built on. Rocque's map of 1769 shows development reaching as far as the south side of Tottenham Street with only Whitefield's Tabernacle lying to the north (built in 1756). A lease was sold to William Gowing, builder, for the north side of Chitty Street in 1776 and it is likely that Charlotte Street and Whitfield Street (then called John Street) were extended northwards to meet it at about the same time.

In 1768 an Act of Parliament was passed to set up the St Pancras West Paving Commission under which 17 commissioners were appointed, including William Goodge and Edmund Pepys, to oversee paving, lighting and street cleaning. They were directed to hold their first meeting at the Two Blue Posts, Tottenham Court Road. The preamble states that 'the pavements of the streets westward of Tottenham Court Road are in a very bad state and in a continual want of repair, and the parish is not duly lighted, cleansed and watched'. The commissioners were empowered to levy rates (6d in the pound for paving, 1/6d for other services) and were directed to put up the names of streets, number the houses, regulate stands for hackney coaches, put up lamps and erect watch houses.

Francis Goodge died in 1771 and his brother William in 1778, whose part of the estate passed to his nephew Samuel Foyster.

Culver Meadow

Although the records are sparse on this part of Fitzrovia, it is known that this field of 12 acres was originally part of the endowment of the pre-Reformation Charterhouse and was recorded in the Commonwealth survey of 1649 as being part of the demesne lands of Tottenhall manor. Its southern boundary ran from the north side of Whitefield's Tabernacle (where a change in the building line of Tottenham Court Road can still be seen), across Chitty Street to Cleveland Street and then north to the centre of the present Maple Street (formerly London Street). By 1657 it was included with land held in Bloomsbury by Thomas, Earl of Southampton. In 1669 it came to the Russell family on the marriage of Rachel Wriothesley with William Russell.

Culver meadow then remained part of the Bedford Estate as tenanted farm land until 1776 when a building lease was granted by Robert Palmer, the Duke of Bedford's agent, who

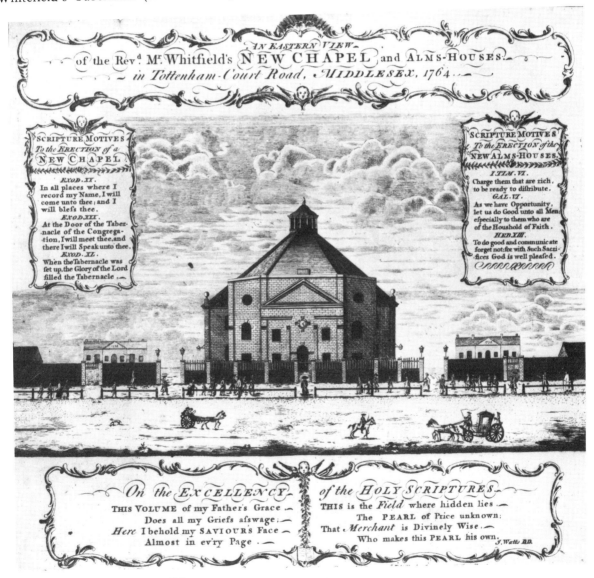

6. *Whitefield's Tabernacle, 1764*

appears to have had a personal interest in the land, to William Gowing, the builder of Chitty Street. The building of good quality houses was completed over the whole area (Howland Street, Russell Place (now the lower part of Fitzroy Street), parts of Cleveland Street and Whitfield Street) by the early 1790s. This area was particularly heavily bombed during the War and nothing remains of the original buildings. The land is now largely taken up by recent developments by the Middlesex Hospital Medical School, the Post Office Tower and the Post Office Headquarters. The few remaining houses on the north side of Maple Street, particularly 14 to 18, were developed by the Southampton Estate and give some indication of how the whole area looked before 1939.

Home Field

This field covered the northern part of Fitzrovia, stretching from Maple Street to Euston Road and Cleveland Street to Tottenham Court Road. Since it was part of the demesne lands of the manor, of which the Fitzroys had acquired the freehold in 1768, there were no intervening leases to prevent the family having full control of its development.

The construction of the New Road in 1756, which had been strongly supported by the Duke of Grafton, helped open up the estate, and the Act of Parliament a decade later gave the Fitzroys the freehold interest which enabled them to sell building leases. It had been the Countess of Arlington who had settled Tottenhall manor on her great-grandson Charles Fitzroy, who was created Lord Southampton in 1780. It was he who married Anne, daughter of Sir Peter Warren, a vice-admiral in the navy (perpetuated in Warren Street). In the closing 30 years of the 18th century Charles Fitzroy played a large part in developing the family lands in a way that was in marked contrast to the southern part of the area so far looked at.

Although no plan of this part of the estate appears to have survived, the Fitzroys gave considerable thought to the planning and layout of Home Field. For Fitzroy Square, the centre-piece of the development, London's most fashionable architects, the Adam brothers, were commissioned to prepare drawings.

Before looking in detail at the development of this square and the streets radiating from it, it is worth noting that building was continuing on the north side of Maple Street in the 1770s, at the same time that the Bedford Estate was completing its development of Culver Meadow. For example in 1777 the Fitzroys granted a building lease on 14, 16 and 18 Maple Street to the Rev. Robert Anthony Bromley. Some years later Bromley also leased the adjoining site on the corner with Whitfield Street for the building of the Fitzroy Chapel. This was completed in 1788 and Bromley became the first incumbent. The *Survey of London* states that 'its design was of the simplest character, of brick, rectangular in plan, with its main axis north and south. The entrance front in Maple Street had a pediment crowned with a bell-cote'. This too fell victim to bombing at the very end of the last War. The north-west end of Maple Street, where it joins Cleveland Street, seems to have been constructed a little later in 1786.

Towards the end of the 1770s development was also taking place on the south side of the east end of Grafton Way. The slightly grander houses on the north side, of which numbers 52 and 54 were leased to builders by William and John Adam, were not begun until 1792. They are therefore contemporary with parts of Fitzroy Square, Conway Street, Warren Street and the north end of Whitfield Street.

The Planned Estate around Fitzroy Square

It is often forgotten that Fitzroy Square was not planned in isolation in the building boom which London experienced in the decade preceding the Napoleonic Wars, but was conceived as part of a planned estate in what was then the fringe of London. As well as the first rate houses of Fitzroy Square, there were houses of lesser quality in surrounding streets, a small shopping centre in Fitzroy Market (now Whitfield Place) and the already existing Fitzroy Chapel in Maple Street. The range of housing designed to attract the middle classes up to the aristocracy, the provision of shops, public houses and a church, with a planned layout by a leading architect fits very much the model that was then being employed on many of the most prestigious estates in the 18th century.

7. *Fitzroy Square*

Surprisingly, very little is known about how Lord Southampton came to commission the Adam brothers to produce drawings for at least two sides of Fitzroy Square and lay out the estate as a whole. On his return from a grand tour of Italy in 1763, Robert Adam established himself in London as the leading classical architect of the period and until his death in 1792, Robert and his brother James completed a large number of schemes for aristocratic clients in town and country. Their best known works in London are probably the Adelphi and the façades of Portland Place. Since Robert Adam's achievements had given him a passport to the most exclusive salons of London, it is very likely that he was well known to Lord Southampton when he was given this, his last major commission before his death.

Fitzroy Square, which is roughly contemporary with Adam's Charlotte Square in Edinburgh, was built in four stages. The east side was begun first in 1792 with leases for 99 years for numbers 2, 9 and 10 in the name of James Adam and numbers 3 to 8 in the names of James and William Adam. So it is clear that Robert Adam's brothers had a direct financial interest in the development. All the houses on this side were fully tenanted in 1798 with the exception of numbers 4, 9 and 10.

The south side of the square was begun a little later in 1794. Numbers 33 to 37 were leased to James Adam, 32 and 34 to James and William Adam and 33 to Thomas Bert, a carpenter. The building of the north and west sides was delayed until 1827-28 and 1832-35 respectively, because of the slump during the Napoleonic Wars. Although only the east and south sides can really be said to be Robert Adam's work, the whole square with its Portland stone or stuccoed façades forms one of London's brightest and most pleasing town squares designed in the classical manner.

The southern section of Conway Street and western part of Grafton Way are contemporary with the east side of Fitzroy Square. Numbers 6, 8 and 10 Conway Street (now converted to flats by Camden Council) were leased to William Adam in 1795. The upper part of Conway Street was completed about five years later. Warren Street was built as a residential street of third rate four storey town houses in 1791-2 — the most typical of surviving Georgian architecture. Number 29 is a particularly fine double-fronted house next to a pub, originally built as the Marquis of Cornwallis. The name of the Prince of Wales Feathers remains unchanged at 8 Warren Street, although the façade was refaced in the early 19th century.

By the end of the 18th century, Horwood's map of London (1799) shows that the whole of Home Field had been completed, apart from the north and west sides of Fitzroy Square, a section of Cleveland Street backing onto Fitzroy Square and part of the north end of Conway Street. These were all completed in the early part of the 19th century.

The East Side of Tottenham Court Road
On this side of Tottenham Court Road the land was as fragmented in ownership as on the west, although as time passed the Bedford Estate bought up parcels of land for building along Gower Street and Torrington Place.

In the north by Euston Road, a thin strip of land was held by the Southampton Estate, which at one time had been part of the field called Murrells, attached to Tottenham Court manor house. This field had been roughly bisected by the New Road and on the southern part Euston Square, the Euston Road frontage as far as Upper Woburn Place and a short turning off Tottenham Court Road called Tottenham Place (now Beaumont Place) were eventually laid out. Of this only the south side of Euston Square survives, having been renamed Endsleigh Gardens in 1879.

To the south of this there were two further fields, forming a square of about 30 acres in total, which were divided from east to west and lying partly in the Parish of St Giles-in-the-Fields. The ownership of these two fields was held separately and seems to have changed hands frequently until they were developed in the late 18th and early 19th centuries.

The northern-most field was in the possession of Hans Winthrop Mortimer of Caldwell, Derbyshire in 1768 but was being farmed by the Capper family, which had lived in the area at least since the late 17th century. By the end of the 18th century this field was known as Brickfields, no doubt reflecting its current usage, when it came into the ownership of Sir William Paxton. By 1800 some development had already been carried out along the Tottenham Court Road frontage and around Mortimer Market and Pancras Street (now Capper Street), and this was gradually extended eastwards to Huntley Street. In 1825 the field was divided into two, the undeveloped eastern section being sold to the founders of the new University College. On this the present building was constructed to a design of William Wilkins.

The southern field of about 9 acres was known as Cantelowe Close and this remained in the ownership of the Holles family, Earls of Clare and later Dukes of Newcastle for nearly 250 years. In 1490 the owner had been Henry Cantelowe and his name was perpetuated in the land. In 1772 the Duke of Newcastle sold Cantelowe Close to Gertrude, Duchess of Bedford and Francis Street (now Torrington Place) was laid out on it.

The Capper family had long been tenant farmers in the area, renting a number of the Duke of Bedford's fields from Tottenham Court Road to what is now Southampton Row. It was in Cantelowe Close, about 150 feet from Tottenham Court Road, just behind Heal's store, that a farmhouse stood from about 1776 until it was demolished in 1914.

Christopher Capper had been the Duke's tenant at least since 1732 and on his death his two daughters, Esther and Mary, continued to run the farm. These two ladies who lived together in a house at the south end of Tottenham Court Road, seemed to have created a formidable impression in the area. In the Bedford Estate records there are several letters from the sisters complaining about the dust on their fields from the New Road — they came out strongly in support of the Duke in his opposition to the road — and about butchers grazing stock in the fields overnight before going to the markets.

J. T. Smith, in his *Book for a Rainy Day*, adds a description of their attempts to deter trespassers:

'They wore riding habits and men's hats; one used to ride with a large pair of shears after boys who were flying their kites, purposely to cut their strings; the other sister's business was to seize the clothes of the lads who trespassed on their premises to bathe'.

References to the Cappers disappear about 1768 and in 1776 the Bedford Estate granted William Mace, a carpenter, a lease for 78 years for a portion of ground 'in consideration of the great expense he hath been at in erecting a farmhouse on part of a field known as Cantelowe Close, and that he, the said William Mace, shall build proper and convenient sheds and other outhouses for the accommodation of 40 cows at the least'. This seems to suggest that Mace constructed the farmhouse after the sisters Capper had given up their tenancy.

John Harris Heal, one of the directors of the family firm, lived in the farmhouse for a number of years until it was demolished in 1914 to make way for an extension to the store and new workshops and warehousing.

The City of London Estate

This is an exceedingly old estate even by the City of London's standards and considerably predates the formation of the Bedford Estate. It is derived from an estate held by John Carpenter, a former Town Clerk of the City of London, who died about 1441. An Act of Parliament in the reign of William IV devoted part of the proceeds from this land to the upkeep of the City of London School.

In 1796 the City Lands sub-committee instructed George Dance, Surveyor to the City of London who lived at 91 Gower Street, to prepare plans for the development of the estate. The ground was then on a long lease to Matthew and Sarah Featherstonhaugh and was not due to revert to the City until 1801. In October 1800 a proposal was put before the sub-committee and eventually approved. The plan was to 'form two crescents at the north and south ends of the said ground and a street to lead from north to south. The houses to be erected thereon to be not less than the second rate of building and to cover the whole front of Tottenham Court Road with buildings adapted for trades and business'. The two crescents were to become North and South Crescent and the street linking them, Alfred Place.

Clearly the development did not match expectations, since the last plots on the east side were not sold until 1805 and in 1809 builders on this side were allowed a year at a peppercorn rent in order to complete and let their houses. The surviving plans and elevations of Dance's proposals show 57 houses of impressive proportions, designed to attract tenants of a high social status. Some minor literary figures like Sheridan Knowles, the dramatist and Thomas Campbell, the poet, lived here in the early part of the century but the aristocracy had generally speaking moved westwards or to outlying villages.

By the middle of the 19th century redevelopment had already begun and by the turn of the century the area was largely one of warehouses, light industries and extensions of the more commercially successful premises facing Tottenham Court Road. The layout of the site remains today exactly how it was planned by Dance but none of the original buildings survive. Alfred Mews, a small cul-de-sac off Tottenham Court Road which was originally the drive to Mace's farmhouse, provided access to stables at the rear of North Crescent. Even today the City of London remains ground landlord of at least some of the land in the area.

Apart from the building of the north and west sides of Fitzroy Square in the 1820s and '30s, the completion of the City of London estate in about 1810 marked the end of the development process in Fitzrovia. Needless to say, this did not mean the area remained static. In the next 150 years it became part of the expanding metropolis, reflecting the changing social and economic fortunes of a capital city. Shops, trades and professions came and went and the successive waves of immigrants from Europe left their mark on the political and cultural life of the area. Fundamentally, it was the availability of cheap accommodation for living and working that enabled Fitzrovia to develop its role as a breeding ground for new ideas in the arts, literature and politics.

Fitzrovia and the Furniture Industry

In the history of London's trades and crafts, Fitzrovia has an unrivalled place as a major centre for cabinet and furniture making. From the mid 18th century, when the area was first developed, through the Victorian heyday of the latter half of the 19th century to the First World War, craftsmen in small workshops around Tottenham Court Road adapted to the changing requirements of the market. The coming of mass-production techniques in purpose-built factories, changes in public taste and the lack of space for expansion in the 1920s and 30s finally forced many small manufacturers to close or to move elsewhere.

Tottenham Court Road's long association with the furniture trade began in the 1750s when a number of craftsmen sought more space and lower rents outside the congested centre of London. In the first half of the century Long Acre and St Martin's Lane had been the main area of production, where for example Chippendale had a workshop. As the demand for good quality furniture increased later in the century, particularly during 'the season', some of the most fashionable manufacturers were to be found on and around Tottenham Court Road. Two of Chippendale's former employees, Copland and Lock, set up shop near Ye Swan, Tottenham Court Road in 1752. Peter Langlois, a specialist in ormolu and inlaid commodes, had a workshop at 2 Stephen Street in 1763, from where he supplied clients such as the Duke of Bedford and Horace Walpole. Another Frenchman, Francis Herve, operated from 32 Lower John Street (now Whitfield Street) from 1785. He supplied a set of French chairs to Lady Spencer at Althorp and built other bespoke items like some library steps, now to be seen at the Victoria and Albert Museum.

These are just a handful of the more distinguished 18th century craftsmen whose trade cards have survived in the Heal collection. It is clear from other sources that there were many other smaller tradesmen and supporting crafts — sawyers, carvers, French polishers and upholsterers — in the neighbourhood at the time. Initially, many of these skills would have been

8. *The calling card of Peter Langlois (from London Furniture Makers 1660-1840 by Ambrose Heal)*

available in the same workshop. As demand increased and skills became more specialised and differentiated, each piece of furniture may well have been transported from one workshop to another until completed. Hence the need for the industry to be concentrated in a small area.

The growth of London's population and a rising demand amongst the middle classes for furniture at a reasonable price brought about a dramatic change in the way the industry was organised. Until about 1840 the process of constructing and selling furniture were closely linked so that it was common practice for the cabinet maker to make and sell articles from the same premises. From the mid-century onwards this system declined and manufacturers began to expand their retail trade while subcontracting the production of furniture to the smaller craftsmen. Increasingly, a series of middle men intervened between the point of production and the point of sale. This ultimately gave rise to the furniture emporia and department stores where furniture to suit all pockets could be purchased off the peg. Many of the larger stores that flourished later in the century — Heal's, Maple's, Catesby's, Thompsons, Shoolbred's — were founded originally by craftsmen. John Harris Heal, the founder of the family dynasty made feather beds and mattresses in Rathbone Place from 1810-18.

Thus for a time the stores of Tottenham Court Road, along with Waring and Gillow's in Oxford Street, had almost complete dominance of the 'respectable' end of the market, and were patronised particularly by those in the rapidly growing Victorian suburbs and expatriots in the colonies. At least one shop, Maple's, went further and experimented with a mail order catalogue.

The rise of the furniture stores in Tottenham Court Road was thus both a development of the earlier craft system and for a time the means of sustaining the industry in the area. Generally speaking, it was Fitzrovia which managed to retain predominance of the, albeit declining, West End bespoke market and the ever expanding good quality ready-made sector. The lower end of the market was catered for almost entirely by the sweated workshops of Curtain Road, Shoreditch and Bethnal Green in the East End.

Although the profits on the retail side were considerable, for the manufacturer overheads and wages had to be pruned to a minimum in order to stay in business. Those doing subcontracted work for the large stores rented the most meagre back yard or mews building and operated on a weekly cycle. As one witness remarked before the House of Lords inquiry on Sweating:

'.... a pound's worth of tools and a second pound in cash starts many 'cabinet-makers' on the career of independent worker, and double that amount will often convert him into an employer."

Saturday was the most important day of the week when an order had to be completed and presented to the store, which often necessitated working through Friday night. Payment was then made and new orders distributed. The piece-master, as he became known, could then pay off his work force and on the following Monday purchase new materials for the next order.

In the 1888 Lords Inquiry into the Sweating System a witness stated:

9. Ambrose Heal

'I have worked for Messrs Maple; and they have always been, to my mind, the one firm for the cabinet trade who have been the pioneers in the sweating system.'

More specifically, they were accused of causing hardship to piece-masters by under paying the agreed price for an order and of paying so late on the Saturday that the craftsman could not get to the bank in time to cash the cheque. Since many local craftsmen depended almost entirely on the large stores for work, Maple's in particular were able to determine not only prices but who was offered work and on what terms. Although the accusation of sweating was not proved in their Lordships' eyes, it was clear that Maples had a large part of the local manufacturing sector under their control and if needs be could always threaten to switch to producers in the Curtain Road area.

St Pancras and Fitzrovia in particular remained a major centre of the furniture trade until the Second World War. Other related trades such as piano making, bed making and picture framing all fluctuated as the market allowed. In 1861 the Census records that there were 3052 people employed in furniture making in St Pancras (12% of the total workforce in the trade in Greater London), but by 1951 this had fallen to 2205 (3.5%). This compares with 3928 and 5092 for Shoreditch in the same two years.

An analysis of Kelly's Street Directory for two sample years, 1863 and 1938, shows that even before the war the industry in Fitzrovia was severely in decline. In 1863 Kelly records 110 addresses specialising in cabinet-making and related trades — upholstering, French polishing and other specialist forms of wood-working. Tottenham Court Road and Charlotte Street had 13 addresses each, Cleveland Street had 10. By 1938 the total figure had fallen to 46, with only one in Tottenham Court Road and six in Charlotte Street. An industry relying on many of the same trades was piano-making and in 1863 there were 18 addresses where pianos were made and/or sold. By 1938 there was only one; most likely a point of sale — J. J. Goddard at 68 Tottenham Court Road.

Fitzrovia provided a cheap, convenient but cramped location for the furniture trade for close on two hundred years. This was just one of the area's many functions as a service area for the West End. The clothing and boot and shoe industries have equally long associations with the area. However, once craft skills began to be replaced by mass production techniques and the process became capital rather than labour intensive, its days were numbered. The workshops first established in the 1750s gave rise to the large department stores of the 1870s and 80s and were in turn supported by them. It was these stores, however, which increasingly stocked the products of the factory system or, like Heals, pioneered the introduction of new styles in different materials from abroad.

In the 1980s both Maple's and Heal's remain intact but all the other large stores have closed, including their rival Waring and Gillow's in Oxford Street. Only one upholsterer survives in Grafton Mews while Louis Koch Ltd. in Cleveland Street now lease their furniture as props for TV and the cinema. Even fewer traces of those who actually worked in the industry survive. Records suggest that the sawyers' union held regular meetings at the Adams' Arms in Conway Street in the 1830s. The Carpenters' Arms in Whitfield Street suggest it may have played a similar role. The fact that the Worshipful Company of Carpenters run a Building Crafts Training School in Great Tichfield Street suggests a long, but as yet unexplored, connection with the area.

The Streets of Fitzrovia

ALFRED MEWS

This is a short mews leading off Tottenham Court Road next to Heal's department store. William Mace, who took over the land once farmed by the Capper family, was granted a lease by the Bedford Estate in 1776 for land in the area to build cattle sheds, after constructing a large farmhouse just behind what is now Heal's shop. In the early 19th century the mews was used as stabling for the houses in nearby Alfred Place and by 1850 Miller's Livery Stables had taken over the mews as a commercial proposition. Thus the mews can be traced back to the driveway for Mace's farmhouse. This was demolished in 1914 to make way for Heal's bedding factory and warehouse which remain in use today.

ALFRED PLACE

Alfred Place which ends in two crescents, North Crescent and South Crescent, was laid out by George Dance the Younger for the City of London Corporation from 1802-10. Four-storey houses were constructed in a classic Georgian style with frontages of 21 feet each. Problems were experienced with the foundations and the development appears to have been too late to be a success, since the gentry had already moved westwards. Chenies Street at the north end and Store Street in the south cut Alfred Place at right-angles and these streets were largely developed by the Bedford Estate. The street pattern survives intact but all the original buildings have been redeveloped. In the 19th century the area was mainly used for light industry and warehousing. In the present century offices and a telephone exchange have appeared; number 19 is one of Richard Seifert's less attractive office blocks in glass and black marble which is rumoured to be the home of the Metropolitan police computer. North Crescent is also graced with an entrance to the bomb shelter constructed in the latter part of the war.

BEDFORD PASSAGE

This runs between 97 Charlotte Street and the back of the Middlesex Hospital Outpatients' Department in Cleveland Street, although the street sign was removed during the recent extension of Astor College, the medical school hall of residence. It formerly marked the boundary between Walnut Tree Field and the Bedford Estate's Culver Meadow. Today it lies immediately north of the last of the eighteenth century houses on the west side of Charlotte Street.

CAPPER STREET

This is a short street, formerly Pancras Street, linking Tottenham Court Road and Huntley Street. It commemorates the Capper family that farmed the area in the early 18th century and was most likely laid out in conjunction with Mortimer Market by Hans Winthrop Mortimer, who then owned the land.

Nos 2-20
Shropshire House

This interesting building with its curved concrete façade looks as though it had connections with a certain French tyre company. It was built in 1932-33 and was occupied by two relatively humble enterprises: Automobile Services Co. Ltd. and Winter Garden Garages. By 1934 the upper floors were let off to a variety of small clothing manufacturers and workshops.

CHARLOTTE PLACE

Fitzrovia has many short passages and courts of which this is one of the most pleasant. It links Goodge Street with Rathbone Street. It is lined by small shops many with long-standing tenants like Eley the fishmonger. William Franks, a local builder who lived at 5 Percy Street, was involved in its development in 1766-67 (roughly contemporary with the rest of Goodge Street), as were Thomas Holmes, a bricklayer, and Thomas Green, a joiner.

CHARLOTTE STREET

Charlotte Street has always been and remains today the focus of Fitzrovia with a wide range of restaurants and shops of many different nationalities. It runs from Rathbone Place to Howland Street. The southern part was begun in the 1760s while the northern end was probably not completed until thirty or forty years later. Charlotte Street was originally built as a residential street but the ground floors were soon converted to shops, coffee houses and other places of refreshment. It is probably named after the popular Queen of George III or just possibly after Charlotte Maria who married the fourth Duke of Grafton in 1784. William Gowing, one of the principal builders of the street also had a daughter ' called Charlotte.

No 1
Peter Violet (born 1749), a painter of miniatures, lived here and exhibited at the Royal Academy from 1790-1819.

No 4
In May 1833 Robert Owen opened the National Equitable Labour Exchange here after being forced to vacate former stables in Grays Inn Road because of a threatened rent increase. The intention was to encourage the development of the co-operative movement by enabling craftsmen to exchange goods and services in the form of labour notes instead of cash. The system proved too inflexible and the Exchange closed in 1834. A school for 100 pupils was also set up here in October 1833, for which half the fees had to be paid in labour notes.

No 7
Janet Brown, an aunt of Charles Dickens by marriage, lived here about 1829.

No 8
Richard Wilson, 'the father of English landscape painting', lived here from 1773-79. He was a founding member of the RA, later its librarian, and died in Tottenham Street. William Woollett (1735-85), who was appointed an historical engraver to the King and whose monument can be seen in Westminster Abbey, occupied rooms in the same house.

10. *Richard Wilson*

No 11
Noel Joseph Desenfans (1745-1807), French picture collector, fine artist and one time Consul-General for Poland, lived here from 1774-1805. Stanislas Augustus, last monarch of Poland, decided in 1790 that he needed a picture collection for his castles and commissioned Desenfans to purchase important paintings in London. In 1795 Poland was annexed and the crown abolished and Desenfans was left with a large collection of paintings. In 1799 he published a plan for a public gallery to display his collection in his house in Charlotte Street. On his death the paintings were to go to his friend Sir Frank Bourgeois on condition that they were housed in a public gallery. Bourgeois commissioned Sir Joan Soane to design a gallery and mausoleum at Dulwich College for the paintings and bodies of Mr and Mrs Desenfans and Bourgeois himself. The latter had already designed a mortuary chapel at the back of his Charlotte Street house because of his obsession with death. In 1814 the Dulwich Gallery opened as the first of its kind allowing full access to the public. It continues as a public gallery today and has recently been redecorated and restored.

11. *Bertorelli's, 1981*

No 14
Esther Capper, daughter of Christopher Capper, farmer of part of the Duke of Bedford's lands lived here from 1770-79.

No 15-17
The Percy Chapel once stood on the site now occupied by Cottrell's, the denture manufacturer. The chapel was built by William Franks in 1765 after obtaining a lease from the Goodge brothers, and this replaced Merchant's waterworks and the windmill which originally occupied the site. The first minister of the chapel was the Rev. Henry Mathew, who was the incumbent for 38 years. For many years he lived at 27 Rathbone Place (q.v.) which was much visited by artists of the time. Mathew retired to 6 Fitzroy Street until his death in 1826. In 1812 J. H. Stewart became minister and in the same year set up a Sunday School and School of Industry at the Chapel. In 1867 the chapel was demolished to be replaced a year later by Cottrell's grand Victorian building. The gas lamps placed outside the main entrance of the building at that time can still be seen today.

No 18
Edward Fitzgerald (1809-83), the eccentric Victorian poet, lived here in 1843 and from 1844-48 at No 60.

No 21
Charles Manning, a sculptor, lived here from 1802-12.

Nos 19-21
Bertorelli's restaurant was founded in 1912 by four brothers from Italy and throughout the 1920s and '30s was popular with artists and writers because of its cheap food. During the war writers such as Dylan Thomas could also be found here when not in the Fitzroy or Wheatsheaf. It has remained a family business and is now managed by Dante Bertorelli, the son of one of the co-founders.

No 30
Charles Dibdin (1754-1814), actor, singer, composer, novelist and author of over 70 operas and musicals, lived here. He later moved to Camden Town and is buried in St Martin's churchyard, now St Martin's Gardens off Bayham Street.

No 32
John Brinsmead, one of the most famous Victorian piano manufacturers with workshops in Windmill Street and then at 15 Charlotte Street, lived here from 1843-52.

No 37
Angelica Catalani (1779-1849), an opera singer and twice director of the Italian Opera in Paris, lived here. She also made frequent appearances at the Tottenham Street theatre (q.v.).

12. *John Constable, self portrait c1800*

No 74

A church was built near the turning with Chitty Street in 1846 at a time when the population of the area was increasing rapidly. St John the Evangelist, as it was called, was designed by Hugh Smith in the then popular Romanesque style. However, it was no beauty and was soundly criticised in a long article in the *Ecclesiologist*. It became the parish church and was linked with a National School in Whitefield Street and an additional one in Whitfield Place. It was badly damaged by a flying bomb in 1945 and was demolished some years later.

No 76

One of the finest houses in Charlotte Street, associated with a succession of artists of national importance, which was demolished soon after the war. Joseph Farington (1747-1821), the landscape artist, lived here from 1780 to his death. He was a friend of George Dance and a pupil of Richard Wilson *(see No 8)*. He was noted for his services to the poor in the recession of 1794-5 and for being a local commissioner for paving and lighting. His Diaries have recently been republished. Farington's friend the painter John Constable moved into the house in 1822 and both lived and worked here until 1837 when he moved to Hampstead. He had previously lodged at No 63 but frequently visited Farington at No 76 during his life-time.

The poet Rupert brooke (1887-1915) also took lodgings here towards the end of 1911 when researching for a dissertation at the British Museum. This won him a fellowship at King's College, Cambridge in 1912. While living here Brooke mixed in Bloomsbury circles with Maynard Keynes, Virginia Woolf and others.

No 81

This house remains substantially unaltered apart from the ground floor and it was here that the architect Sir Robert Smirke spent most of his younger years. He was also baptised at the Percy Chapel in October 1781. He is best known for designing the British Museum (1823-47), although he was one of the most prolific architects of the early 19th century, completing a large number of public and private commissions. In 1813 he was made one of three official architects to the Board of Works with Soane and Nash.

13. *Robert Smirke*

14. *Joseph Farington, from an original picture by T. Lawrence*

15. No 76 Charlotte Street

No 85

Here Daniel Maclise, the historical painter and friend of Dickens, lived from 1835-37. In later years he achieved considerable fame as a painter and in 1857 was commissioned to paint frescoes in the House of Lords. He later moved to 4 Cheyne Walk where he died.

No 98

When William Goodge died in 1778 his part of the estate passed to his nephew Samuel Foyster. Ann Foyster, a descendant of the latter, lived here from 1812-26 and four years later the Rev. John Goodge Foyster was also resident until 1833.

No 107

Between 1902-18 rooms were used in this house for meetings of the Communist Club after it moved from the basement of 49 Tottenham Street. Speakers at the club read almost like a *Who's Who* of radical politics — Marx, Engels, Bernard Shaw, Keir Hardy, William Morris, Sidney Webb and the anarchist bomber Johann Most. The club was closed down after a police raid in 1918.

In the mid 1930s the singer Peter Pears lodged in Charlotte Street with a friend Peter Burra, a journalist on the *Times*, where they were visited several times by Benjamin Britten.

CHITTY STREET

This short street links Charlotte Street and Whitfield Street but nothing remains of the original buildings. It was formerly called North Street and is now named after Thomas Chitty (1802-78), a special pleader and legal writer. He was the second son of Joseph Chitty (1776-1841), a legal writer who lived and died in Conway Street. From 1836-66 Thomas Chitty lived at 104 Gower Street and is best known for editing standard law books and for writing Forms of Practical Proceedings (Chitty's Forms).

CLEVELAND STREET

Named after Charles II's mistress the Duchess of Cleveland whose son became Henry Fitzroy, Cleveland Street was originally called Upper Newman Street (later Norfolk Street) from Goodge Street to Tottenham Street and Cleveland Street northwards to the Euston Road. Before the area was developed it was a farm track called the Green Lane, dividing St Pancras from St Marylebone, and leading to Farthing Pie House now the Green Man on the Euston Road. The borough boundary originally extended down Cleveland Street (as it does today) and crossed Goodge Street between numbers 59 and 61 and continued down

16. *Middlesex Hospital c1835*

the back of Newman Street to Rathbone Street. Today it turns left at the end of Cleveland Street, goes down the centre of Goodge Street as far as Charlotte Place, where it now turns down to Rathbone Street.

Cleveland Street has never been very prepossessing and has always suffered from being a narrow but much used thoroughfare between Goodge Street and the Euston Road. It was developed gradually from south to north and crosses at least three of the original landholdings in the area. Most of the houses were originally built for residential purposes but only No 120 survives intact. The majority were converted to shops or workrooms on the ground floor early in the 19th century. Nos 16, 18 and 20 are good examples of this.

From the beginning, however, Cleveland Street suffered from the expansion of the Middlesex Hospital on the west side and the building of the Covent Garden Workhouse on the east (this is now the Hospital Outpatients' department). In the late 19th century its reputation was given a fatal blow by the exposure of the gay bordello at No 19, which nearly caused a constitutional crisis because it was frequented by the future Duke of Clarence, who was in direct line to the throne.

The Middlesex Hospital was founded in Windmill Street in 1745 but in order to expand land was purchased from the Berners Estate on its present site. Building began in 1755 but it took a further 20 years for the new hospital to be completed to the design of architect James Paine.

Gardens originally backed onto Riding House Street and a terrace of houses extended down the west side of Cleveland Street, but these were lost in later phases of expansion. The present building was reconstructed on the original H plan in the 1920s, much of it paid for by private subscription. The hospital and medical school have always had a considerable reputation in the medical world and over the last two centuries have benefited from private and philanthropic legacies. Many have cause to be grateful for treatment received at the hospital while for others, like Rudyard Kipling, Hugh Gaitskell and more recently Peter Sellers, nothing could be done.

No 7

Possibly the most important Victorian artistic school was formed here when in 1848 Dante Gabriel Rossetti wrote to Holman Hunt asking if he could share his studio because he so much admired his work. For some years a close relationship developed between the two painters and the Pre-Raphaelite Brotherhood was born. The partnership suffered an immediate setback when Hunt fell into rent arrears and Rossetti had to move to a studio at 27 Newman Street.

No 19

This house has long since been displaced by the Middlesex Hospital but its reputation lives on in the events surrounding it which nearly caused a constitutional crisis. In July 1889 police uncovered a rather sordid homosexual brothel whereby young Post Office clerks were procured for the pleasures of the well-to-do by the proprietor Charles Hammond. It soon became clear that Lord Arthur Somerset, Lord Euston, the local landowner, and the bisexual grandson of Queen Victoria, Prince Albert Victor (Eddy) were all regular customers. Queen Victoria was personally informed and on her instructions an immediate cover-up was instituted by the then prime minister, Lord Salisbury. Key witnesses and defendants were silenced or allowed to flee abroad. In addition, a libel suit was hurriedly concocted against Ernest Parke, the editor of the *North London Press,* who dared to suggest that justice had been miscarried.

No 20

As a result of detailed detective work, it has recently been suggested that the real reason for the cover-up of the Cleveland Street brothel was not so much to prevent publication of the facts but to prevent an earlier cover-up linking prince Eddy with the street being exposed. This scandal was potentially far more dangerous to the establishment and its very pinnacle, the monarchy. It is argued by Stephen Knight in *'Jack the Ripper: The Final Solution'* that young prince Eddy had become a ward of the painter Walter Sickert because of his artistic leanings and had got to know Annie Elizabeth Crook, who worked in a tobacconist's shop at 20 Cleveland Street and lived in the basement of No 6. In 1885 they had an illegitimate daughter, Alice Margaret, and married secretly soon after. Since Annie was Roman Catholic, a commoner and mother of the prince's illegitimate daughter, the authorities panicked and in 1888 launched a police raid on the basement taking Eddy back to the safety of the palace while Annie was committed to a mental institution. Mary Kelly, a witness at the wedding, and the baby escaped to the East End. Knight argues convincingly that the five 'Jack the Ripper' murders which terrorised the East End from August to November 1889, one of whom was Mary Kelly, were carried out with the full knowledge of the Home Secretary to remove all witnesses and others who knew about the royal wedding. One of the less convincing but more fascinating parts of the book is Knight's attempt

to link the Ripper murders to a plot by masons to defend the name of the Crown, and perpetrated by Sir William Gull, mason and Royal physician, John Netley, Royal coachman and Walter Sickert himself.

No 22

The parents of Charles Dickens took lodgings with a family here (then 10 Norfolk Street) when they first moved to London in 1814-16. Dickens returned to live at this house between 1829-31 and then took lodgings at 15 (now 25) Fitzroy Street for a short time. Dickens was later to use 'Green Lanes', the original name for Cleveland Street, as a setting where part of the mob seek refuge after the Gordon Riots in his novel *Barnaby Rudge.* The description of the area in Chapter 44 is colourful rather than accurate.

Nos 88-90

Before this section of the street had been developed a deep pit covered the area and in 1799 an unfortunate accident befell the Earl of Scarborough and his sister Lady Louisa Hartley. On the way back to her home in Gower Street their coach left the road and ended up in the pit. The occupants of the coach survived shaken but uninjured but the coachman and footman received serious injuries, the latter dying after having a leg amputated.

No 106

Louis Koch Ltd. now hire out antique furniture to the cinema and television industry and behind this façade have a wide range of props, some of them genuine antiques. The firm was founded here by German-born Louis Koch in the 1920s and for 30 years he restored antique furniture and built reproduction models. It was his son George who expanded the firm into its present line of business and took over adjoining premises in Fitzroy Mews, Warren Mews and 22 Fitzroy Square for storage and repairs.

No 141

Samuel Morse, the American painter and inventor of the Morse code, lived here from 1812-15.

COLVILLE PLACE

An alleyway linking Charlotte Street and Whitfield Street which until the war was lined on both sides by small terraced houses. Now half the southern side has been bombed or demolished to make way for a car park. The houses were originally constructed by John Colville, a carpenter, in the 1770s, but most have been subsequently altered. Some still have early 19th century shopfronts intact. Colville himself lived here in 1783.

No 20

One of the houses bombed during the war, this was once a pub called the Rose and Crown. Theatrical performances took place here in the early 19th century.

No 22

George Gissing, then an unknown writer, lodged here from January to September 1878. He is best known as the author of *New Grub Street*, which makes frequent references to the then grim area west of Tottenham Court Road. In his partly autobiographical book, *The Private Papers of Henry Ryecroft*, Gissing writes:

'I see that alley (Colville Place) hidden on the west side of Tottenham Court Road where, after living in a back bedroom on the top floor, I had to exchange for a front cellar. There was a difference, if I remember rightly, of sixpence a week, and sixpence in those days was a great consideration — why it meant a couple of meals.'

CONWAY STREET

This is an attractive street of Georgian houses which has survived almost intact. In the latter part of the 19th century it was called Southampton Street but in the present century it reverted to its original name. The Post Office Directory of 1863 records that the Southampton Estate office was at No 1 and No 7 was for many years the head office of Bishop's, the removers, whose stables still survive, but which are soon to be demolished, just off Carburton Street. The Adams Arms was part of the original Southampton Estate development and in the 1830s was used as a meeting place of two craft unions: the marble polishers and sawyers.

Bromley Place and Conway Mews off the south end of Conway Street were no doubt built for carriages and stabling in the original development, but none of the original buildings survive.

CYPRESS PLACE

Originally a mews linking the eastern end of Howland Street and Maple Street; after the redevelopment of this block only the name survives.

EUSTON ROAD (Nos 293-375)

When the New Road from Paddington to Islington was planned most of the road was lined with terraces of large houses with front gardens of at least 50 feet, since in the original Act of Parliament no development was allowed within this distance from the highway. These houses have entirely disappeared and the front gardens have been taken up in successive road widening schemes and redevelopment. This stretch of the Euston Road survived the last road widening scheme by the LCC in the early 1960s but the few surviving shops, restaurants and the former Post Office, which recently housed the Open Space theatre are now under threat of redevelopment by a large property company. By the end of the 18th century this part of the road became known for the many monumental masons and specialists in statuary who could meet the requirements of all pockets without too much regard for the finer art of Flaxman, Nollekens and the like. This part of the road therefore became known as Quickset Row, after the artificial stone cement that was commonly used.

No 357

The first soup kitchen in London was founded here by Isaac Negus Jackins in 1846 as a gesture to the poor and destitute that populated the area at the time. The premises were rebuilt in 1873 and were still operating in 1902. The annual report for 1901 preserved in the Heal Collection records that between November and April of that year 63,000 of the poor were supplied with food, which included servings of plum pudding at Christmas.

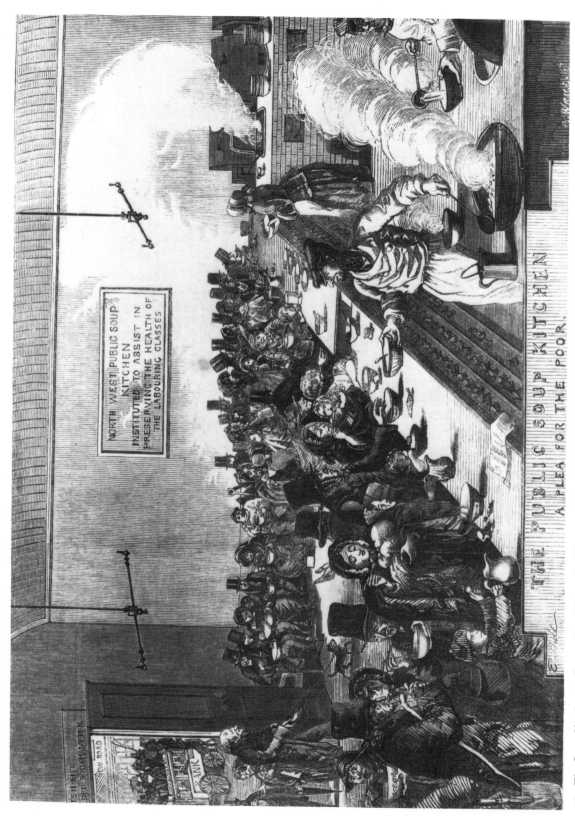

17. The Soup Kitchen in Euston Road (from the Illustrated Times 18 Dec 1858)

FITZROY COURT

A narrow court running from Tottenham Court Road, under the former Grafton Hotel and Newton Works, to Whitfield Place. In the early 19th century it was called Holbrook Buildings with Holbrook Court running northwards from it. Later in the century some tenement buildings stood on the site which were demolished in 1908. In the 1930s Fitzroy Court was lined by small shops such as Rosetti & Co., musical instrument makers, a printer and a commercial photographer. These have all been vacant for some years.

FITZROY MEWS

A former mews behind Fitzroy Square, it is now almost entirely taken up with storage space for Louis Koch Ltd. *(see 106 Cleveland Street).*

FITZROY SQUARE

Architecturally one of London's finest squares, Fitzroy Square has always had to struggle to maintain its reputation as a sought-after address. Throughout the first half of the 19th century it could boast a considerable number of residents of social and artistic importance but towards the end of the century succumbed to a number of anonymous commercial hotels, private schools and bohemian artistic menàges. The square reached its lowest point at the turn of the century and when Virginia Stephen (before marrying Leonard Woolf) sought cheap rooms to share with her brother she went so far as to inquire of the police whether they would be safe living in the square. It was heavily bombed in the last war and after reconstruction offices quickly took over. Today there are no more than a handful of residents left with only two houses in residential use.

The *Survey of London* lists large numbers of almost totally forgotten Victorian artists as having lived here. The most notable of the former residents are:

No 2

Sir Frank Dicksee, artist, lived here in 1896.

No 6

Sir William Orchardson, the subject painter, lived here from 1862-71.

Between 1874-88 the house was occupied by the Dicksee family, at least four members of which were painters. The artist Alexander Melville lived here from 1890-92, having previously lived at No 34.

No 7

Sir Charles Eastlake, an artist of considerable stature in the Victorian era, president of the RA and Director of the National Gallery, lived here from 1849-65. Previously, in 1831-43, he lived at 39 Fitzroy Street. His wife, who survived him, remained at No 7 until 1893.

No 11

Robert Edis (1838-1927) lived here from 1871-1900. He was the architect of buildings such as the Great Northern Hotel at Marylebone, the Great Eastern Hotel and Liverpool Street station and The Place, Duke Street, formerly the headquarters of the 38th Middlesex (Artists) Rifle Volunteers of which he was a member. With the formation of the LCC, Edis was elected a member for St Pancras South.

No 21

Baronet Gascoyne Cecil, 3rd Marquis of Salisbury, Secretary of State for India in 1874, Foreign Secretary in 1878, Prime Minister in 1885-6, 1886-92 and 1895-1902, lived here briefly after his marriage in 1857. He spent much of his time at his ancestral home, Hatfield House.

In 1909 Maynard Keynes, the economist, and Duncan Grant, the artist and designer, shared rooms here while Keynes had a fellowship at King's College Cambridge. They were frequent visitors to No 29 where Virginia Stephen and her brother Adrian lived at the time.

No 29

George Bernard Shaw lived here from 1887, when he moved in with his mother, to 1898, when he married Charlotte Payne-Townshend. He was music and drama critic for several papers, writer of political and economic tracts for the Fabian Society, which he joined in 1884, and author of several unsuccessful novels before achieving considerable success as a dramatist. After his marriage he moved to 10 Adelphi Terrace.

On the death of their father Leslie, the Stephen

18. Virginia Woolf, from a photograph by G. C. Beresford

children moved to 46 Gordon Square in 1904. When Vanessa Stephen married Clive Bell in 1907, Virginia and her brother Adrian took rooms at this address until 1911. Here they held regular 'Thursday evenings'; a custom which had developed when at Gordon Square. Duncan Grant, Maynard Keynes, Leonard Woolf, Lytton Strachey and Lady Ottoline Morrell formed the nucleus of this Bloomsbury outpost. In 1911 Virginia and Adrian moved to 38 Brunswick Square, sharing rooms with Maynard Keynes, Duncan Grant and Leonard Woolf.

No 33

It was here that Roger Fry set up the Omega Studios in 1913 with Vanessa Bell to support and encourage the work of impecunious young artists and designers and to introduce the ideas of the Post-Impressionists to England. For several years Omega was unique as a centre for creativity in all aspects of design and became a focus for artistic activity in London just before the First World War. In 1915 a faction under the influence of Percy Wyndham Lewis left Omega after a disagreement over a commission for the Ideal Home Exhibition, which led to the formation of the Vorticist movement. Omega's contribution to the field of Post-Impressionist design and decoration in painting, furniture and upholstery has undergone something of a renaissance in recent years and is now recognised as a particularly English response to an international movement, which has been for too long undervalued.

No 37

The Pre-Raphaelite painter Ford Madox Brown (1821-93), father of the novelist Ford Madox Ford, lived here in the 1870s. He was known as a slightly eccentric artist whose house became a frequent meeting place for the Brotherhood. This house was used by William Thackeray as the residence of Colonel Newcome and is described in his novel *The Newcomes*.

During the First World War the first floor was occupied by Walter Taylor, the water colourist, friend and collector of the works of Walter Sickert.

19. George Bernard Shaw

No 38

Sir William Ross, the painter of miniatures, lived here till his death in 1860.

No 40

William De Morgan, the ceramicist and novelist who was born in 1839 at 69 Gower Street, shared this house with James Tennent Lyon from 1865-72, and collaborated in designing and making stained glass. De Morgan is perhaps better known for his attractive ceramic tiles. In 1872 the kiln caused a small fire in the house and the two artists were evicted the same year. This house, together with the former Omega Studios are now merely appendages to the National Foot Hospital.

Two further notable residents of the square, whose precise addresses are unknown, are

Thomas Butts, a patron and friend of William Blake and Francis Dodd (1874-1949), a painter of landscapes and portraits. Dodd moved to London from Glasgow in 1904 when he became a member of the New English Art Club.

FITZROY STREET

Fitzroy Street is a continuation of Charlotte Street running northwards from Howland Street as far as the Euston Road. Sadly little remains of the fine Georgian houses that lined both sides of the street. Many suffered irreparable bomb damage; others were cleared after the war to make way for large and anonymous office blocks. An indication of how the street must have looked can be seen from the surviving houses at the north end — especially Nos 39-43 and the short terrace of Nos 25-37.

Throughout the 19th century and up to 1945 artists sought lodgings, rooms and studios, according to their circumstances, in these large rambling houses — many now of national or international standing. One house, No 8, provided accommodation to an astonishing succession of artists over at least 50 years.

No 4

Dr David Daniel Davis, a leading obstetrician who became a consultant to the Duchess of Kent at the birth of the future Queen Victoria in 1817, moved from Wales to Charlotte Street in 1812. Most of his life was spent at this address while he held the post of obstetric physician at University College Hospital. Having lived for a time at 5 Fitzroy Square he died at 6 Fitzroy Square in 1841.

No 8

This house, a photo of which fortunately survives, seems to have been let as rooms or studios from the end of the 19th century and was used by a succession of notable artists, mainly as a studio and meeting place, less often as a residence.

In 1863 the house was occupied by two surgeons by the name of Ellis but soon after was taken over by Mrs Hill and her two daughters, one of whom was Octavia Hill, as the premises for a Ladies' Guild, a somewhat strange off-shoot of

20. *No 8 Fitzroy Street, 1950, with a memorial tablet to Octavia Hill*

the Christian Socialists, to teach girls to design and paint on glass. Octavia Hill went on to play a leading role in the field of housing reform — much of her work in visiting and rent collection being done in this area — and in helping to establish the National Trust.

By the end of the 19th century 8 Fitzroy Street became associated with the artistic community in Fitzrovia. In 1895 James McNeil Whistler lived and worked here before moving to Hampstead.

Walter Sickert had been an assistant of Whistler until 1882. On his return from France Sickert took over Whistler's old studio in 1907 and established an open house for like-minded artists on Sunday afternoons. Sickert and other local artists soon formalised their relationship into a series of shifting groups — the Fitzroy Street

21. Walter Sickert and his wife, a photograph by Cecil Beaton in 1940

Group, the Camden Town Group and the London Group, all of which met at rooms rented for the purpose at 19 Fitzroy Street. These groups, and Sickert especially, played a leading role in developing the British school of impressionist art in the years leading up to the First World War. It is perhaps surprising that members of these groups painted many portraits in Fitzroy Street and interior views, but very little of the immediate vicinity as they did of Camden Town.

A friend of Sickert at the time describes the studio named after the first artist to use it thus:

'The Whistler ... was a huge room at the back of the first floor of that vast rambling rookery of a house; one reached it by winding passages and steps turning odd corners that seemed to double on themselves; strangers seldom managed to find their way through the labyrinth without assistance. But when one did finally arrive, the picture was unexpected. One was transplanted suddenly from the mundane present to the heart of the eighteenth century. Number 8 had been of no account for years; it was not worth anyone's while to interfere with the character of the place, so that its atmosphere was unchanged. I doubt if there was another room with more echoes of the Georgian era in London. Spacious, beautifully proportioned, rather dark, with long windows looming through the dusk and misty looking-glasses on the high walls, it held secrets that were all its own.'

(M. Lilly. Sickert: The Painter and his Circle. Elek, 1971.)

In 1919 Paul Nash, the painter, stayed here briefly and in the 1920s and '30s Vanessa Bell and Duncan Grant, both artists connected with the Omega Studios and important members of the Bloomsbury Group, had a studio here.

No 9

Edmund Pepys lived here from 1808-12. Pepys helped finance the development of Colville Place and other parts of the Charlotte Street area and was one of the first members of the St Pancras West Paving Commission. In 1818 his daughter Charlotte is recorded as living in the house.

No 12

William Coldstream, painter and member of the Euston Road School, occupied the ground floor flat in the late 1930s. The Euston Road School was founded in 1937 at the School of Drawing and Painting at 316 Euston Road by Coldstream, Victor Pasmore and Claude Rogers.

Elisabeth Lutyens, composer and daughter of Edwin Lutyens, lived here 1938-39 after marrying Edward Clark. They later lived at No 6 from 1942-57 when the house was demolished. Elisabeth Lutyens mixed in artistic and musical circles at the Fitzroy, Wheatsheaf and the George, Mortimer Street and in 1944 rented the top floor of her flat to Dylan Thomas and his wife Caitlin for a few months — not without some disturbance to other tenants in the house.

An earlier occupant of the house had been Simeon Solomon, an influential writer and artist in the Aesthetic Movement.

No 15

W. P. Frith, the Victorian painter, had a studio here where he painted one of his most famous

22. Dylan Thomas, charcoal, by Michael Ayrton 1945

canvases, *Derby Day*. The same studio was rented by Walter Sickert, who sought inspiration by renting many different rooms and studios in areas such as Fitzrovia and Camden Town.

No 18

Augustus John, the portrait painter, whose bohemian temperament matched exactly that of Fitzrovia, lived and worked in this house between 1901-06. In 1907 he also had a studio in 8 Fitzroy Street. John's studio was later used by the painter Henry Lamb and Albert Rutherston, an associate of Sickert and a member of the Fitzroy Street Group.

No 20

This was occupied for a time by three Victorian poets: Lionel Johnson, Victor Parr and Selwyn Image.

No 21

Spencer Gore, one of the founder members of the Fitzroy Street Group and friend of Sickert had a studio here. In 1911 he became the first president of the Camden Town Group. Roger Fry, with Vanessa Bell the leading inspiration behind the Omega Studios, also had a studio here.

No 23

James Playfair, the father of the 18th century Edinburgh architect William Playfair, took a lease on Nos 21 and 23 in 1788 to his death in 1794.

No 38

David Roberts, a minor Victorian painter, lived here from 1840-64. He was more prolific than successful and exhibited 90 paintings at the Royal Academy while resident in Fitzroy Street.

No 39

Sir Charles Eastlake lived here from 1831-43 before moving to 7 Fitzroy Square (c.f.). This house survives intact and has been carefully restored by Camden Council.

23. Augustus John, chalk drawing, self portrait c1901

24. Sir Charles Eastlake

No 54

Captain Matthew Flinders R.N. (1774-1814), explorer and navigator of Australasia lived here.

No 60

Formerly the Goat and Compasses public house, designed by W. M. Brutton in 1896, this building is now given over to commercial uses. Brutton designed the Fitzroy Tavern in Charlotte Street the following year.

Others who have lived in Fitzroy Street include the artist Robert Sargent Austin and the novelist and critic, V. S. Pritchett, who borrowed a friend's room here to finish a book some time in the 1930s.

GOODGE PLACE

Originally called Cumberland Street and after 1881 Little Goodge Street, Goodge Place is an interesting by-way which links Goodge Street and Tottenham Street. It is made up of two terraces of quite small mid 18th century houses with interesting doorcases, which would probably have been considered 'fourth rate' by Georgian standards. Their survival is particularly fortunate in that they remain almost entirely unaltered to the present day, both internally and externally, and because London has relatively few surviving houses of this type, as opposed to the larger better quality houses which can be found in Fitzrovia and elsewhere.

It is often found that houses that have consistently provided low quality multi-occupied accommodation survive with remarkably few alterations to the fabric. Goodge Place is just such an example. It is clear from the census that Goodge Place has been heavily multi-occupied at least from 1841 and probably since it was built.

The fact that Goodge Place is still standing is due more to luck and local action than the powers of conservation. In the 1950s the LCC put a closing order on the east side because they were unfit but neglected to acquire them for demolition, although a number of houses were decanted and boarded up. In the early 1970s the Middlesex Hospital proposed to redevelop the street for a new outpatients' department but this was dropped through lack of finance. Some years

later Camden Council with local pressure served a compulsory purchase order on Nos 8-14 and although two were excluded, renovation work is now proceeding slowly.

To give an example of the extent of overcrowding in these houses which even now lack bathrooms or inside w.c.s and which have very dark low-ceilinged basements, a look at the returns for the 1841 census is instructive. At that time there were 27 houses each with four floors and a basement, containing ten rooms per house. The census shows that in 1841 these 27 houses were occupied by a total of 485 people, made up of 125 families with two or more members and 64 single people. This means that each house contained an average of 18 people with almost two people per room. The most densely occupied house contained 32 people. When it is remembered that many occupants also carried on trades such as dressmaking in the same room, the extent of squalor and overcrowding can just about be imagined. The 1863 Post Office Directory lists 12 addresses in the street where trades were being pursued, including the King's Head pub at No 7 and a baker at No 27, so the living space must have been further reduced.

In 1938 there was a fishmonger at No 14 (the shopfront is still visible) and next door at No 39 Tottenham Street was a grocer which later became a glass shop; it is now the home of the Fitzrovia Neighbourhood Association.

GOODGE STREET

Tallis describes Goodge Street in 1838 as being 'a broad open street, of great thoroughfare, conducting to the Middlesex Hospital and Charles Street, and entirely composed of respectable retail shops'. Its functions as both a thoroughfare and as a street of shops continue today.

From the 1760s until 1939 the shopfronts were occupied by an ever changing succession of grocers, wine merchants, tobacconists and milliners, which only began to be displaced by restaurants, cafes and kebab houses after 1945. Even today those shops which have survived still display the variety which has always characterised the street. The importance of Goodge Street as a shopping centre was reinforced by a street market held on Fridays and Saturdays which is referred

25. *Goodge Street, 1981*

to in Walford's *Old and New London* written in the late 19th century.

On the north corner with Tottenham Court Road, Catesby's had a large house-furnishing store in the 1920s and '30s, which has now been partly replaced by Tesco's, but part of the original building survives on the corner of Tottenham Court Road. On the south corner opposite — now replaced by a shoe shop — stood the Talbot public house, which like most of the other pubs in the street — the Valiant Trooper, the Northumberland Arms and the One Tun — date back to the origins of the street.

At least one notable historical event took place in the street. On 27th June 1777 the Rev. William Dodd was executed at Tyburn for forging a bond for £4,200 in the name of a former pupil, the Earl of Chesterfield. Before facing the gallows, Dodd appealed to Dr Johnson to seek clemency on his behalf but this proved fruitless. Dodd's body was taken to the shop of Mr Davies, an undertaker, in Goodge Street in the hope that he could be revived. The famous surgeon, John Hunter was summoned as he had had some success in cases of drowning. Despite a hot bath and other prescriptions, Dodd's body was carried from the shop feet first.

GRAFTON MEWS

A typical London mews which originally had stabling on the ground floor with small flats above for coachmen, stable boys and the like. A few of these survive but all changed to other uses. The mews connects Grafton Way with Warren Street.

GRAFTON WAY

The western section, from Cleveland Street to Tottenham Court Road, survives almost intact with a number of fine houses (Nos 56-62), well preserved but awaiting improvement. The eastern section, from Tottenham Court Road to Gower Street has very little to recommend it with the new Maple's development on the north side and the site of the former Shoolbred's department store, now a car park, on the south side.

No 12

Algernon Swinburne, the Victorian poet, lived here briefly in 1861/2, having previously lived at 77 Newman Street.

No 58

Here lived Francisco De Miranda (1756-1816), Venezuelan born founder of a masonic lodge in London and leader and source of inspiration for the liberation of Venezuela and indeed much of Latin America, from 1803-10. In 1810 he met here Venezuela's first diplomatic mission led by Simon Bolivar and returned soon after to lead the struggle for the liberation of his own country. He was captured by the Spanish in 1812 and died a prisoner in Cadiz in 1816. This house has been acquired by the Venezuelan Government and plans exist to convert it to a museum as part of a larger cultural centre.

26. *Francisco De Miranda*

No 72
The Grafton Arms.

A pub with an attractive façade, which dates back to the building of the Southampton Estate. From November 1877 to February 1878 meetings of the Social Democratic Club, one of the many radical political groups which flourished in the area, were held here on Sunday evenings. The Club was formed by Frank Kitz to link foreign radicals and British artisans and met originally in the Spread Eagle, Mortimer Street. In 1879 it moved to 6 Rose Street (now Manette Street, off Charing Cross Road) with Kitz as secretary of the English section.

GRESSE STREET

Originally a street of Georgian houses and workshops running from Rathbone Place and ending in a cul-de-sac just to the north of Hanway Place, it is now merely a service road to the EMI office development.

No 31

The Bricklayers' Arms was a secluded pub off the beaten track, now vacant and undergoing renovation. During the war years it was known as the Burglars' Rest supposedly because a gang had once broken in over a weekend and drunk the place dry.

HANWAY PLACE

Once called Petty's Court after Petty's Old Playhouse, which was here in 1736 according to the *London Daily Post* of the time. It still retains much of its character as a narrow, early 18th century street. The change in ownership between this piece of land and the Gort Estate to the north can still be clearly seen since Hanway Place is built right up to the boundary with blank walls.

No 5

Westminster Jews Free School; the former school building, rebuilt in 1882, survives but after conversion to different uses. The name is still visible on the front.

HANWAY STREET

This runs between Oxford Street and Tottenham Court Road and while the Oxford Street side has been largely redeveloped it still has many original buildings surviving on the north side. In the 18th century it was the main route to Oxford Street from the west and Bloomsbury via Great Russell Street and became well known for its lace shops and milliners and in this respect pre-dated Oxford Street for the sale of clothing and fashions. In 1805 William Godwin, the novelist, philosopher and father-in-law of the poet Shelley, had a bookshop here.

HOWLAND STREET

This was a street of respectable houses in the late 18th and early 19th centuries, all of which have now disappeared to be replaced by the Post Office Headquarters, the Post Office Tower and a large number of office blocks. In the early 19th century it was inhabited by aspiring artists of little consequence, none of whom compared with the former residents of Fitzroy Street. Thackeray used it for the lodging of Clive Newcome in '*The Newcomes*'

27. *Hanway Street 1981*

and in the 1930s Nina Hamnett, a painter and illustrator once connected with the Omega Studios lived in a house in this street called Thackeray House.

No 27
Now covered by the Middlesex Hospital Medical School. J. R. Dicksee, artist and uncle of the more famous Frank Dicksee lived here.

No 35
Paul Verlaine and Arthur Rimbaud, two French poets, shared lodgings here in 1872-3. Verlaine went on to become a leading member of the Symbolist movement and dominated the cultural life of Paris's left bank in the 1890s.

HUNTLEY STREET
Running parallel to Tottenham Court Road on the east side, Huntley Street has a few surviving early 19th century houses at the north end. At the south end are the flats, originally built by the Metropolitan Police in 1908, which for a time housed the largest squat in London, before they were evicted to make way for the much disputed nurses' home.

KIRKMAN PLACE
A short alley off Tottenham Court Road next to the police station (No 55) which once led to the St John the Evangelist National Schools. This was a large school building, which also fronted onto Whitfield Street, built in the mid 19th century under the aegis of the church of the same name in Charlotte Street. It was most probably bombed in the war and was replaced with an office block.

MAPLE PLACE
A rear service yard running off Maple Street; 9-18 Maple Place is a Victorian industrial building of some size quite possibly used by the furniture store. It is now a supplies depot for the Post Office.

MAPLE STREET
Once a street with houses very similar to those in Howland Street, Maple Street likewise housed the aspiring rather than the successful. The Fitzroy Chapel stood on the north west corner with Whitfield Street until it was bombed in 1945 and has been replaced by a hall of residence for the University of London.

At the west end stands the Post Office Tower and telecommunications complex which still attracts large numbers of visitors although as of 1980 even the revolving restaurant has been closed to the public. The tower is one of the few buildings designed by the former Ministry of Public Building and Works which is highly praised by architectural critics. It stands 580 feet high surmounted by a 40 foot radio mast and was completed in 1968. A bomb placed in the tower by the IRA in 1971 resulted in the public viewing gallery being closed leaving only the highly priced restaurant run by the Butlin organisation open to those who could afford it. This was closed because, it was said, the high-speed lifts needed replacing.

Maple Street was named after Sir Blundell Maple, MP for Dulwich, whose family owned Maple's store in Tottenham Court Road. The business began when John Maple and James Cook, brothers-in-law who both married sisters called Blundell, acquired in 1841 what was called the Tottenham Cloth Hall in Tottenham Court Road. For four years they worked in partnership as wholesale drapers and warehousemen, later adding bedding and carpets to their stock. In 1845 John Maple took over the whole concern and began to expand it as a family business. In the latter part of the 19th century Maple's contracted out a large part of their furniture-making and upholstery to local craftsmen and soon developed a reputation for driving a hard bargain. This was helped by the fact that their growth was such that they soon had a near monopoly of the cheap end of the furniture market.

In 1888 Maple's were called upon to justify their sub-contracting methods before the House of Lords Sub-Committee on the Sweating System (1888 vol. XX) and in the event even Sir John Blundell Maple felt compelled to appear before the sub-committee to uphold the family name. In

28. Post Office Tower from Fitzroy Street 1981

29. Rear of Maple Street 1981.

the end the case was not proven either way, but the lengthy investigations of witnesses has meant that a wealth of information about the furniture trade has survived.

MIDFORD PLACE

A small turning off the north end of Tottenham Court Road; the origin of the name is unknown. Ambrose Heal in the *London Furniture Makers* 1660-1840, records that a chairmaker called James Finlayson worked here from 1794-1803.

MORTIMER MARKET

Once the site of a market as the name implies, today the square survives but is entirely surrounded by new building, including the UCH Dental Hospital.

NORTH COURT

A small court off Chitty Street with one 19th century workshop surviving which was once occupied by a bed maker.

PERCY MEWS

A narrow mews leading off Rathbone Place next to the Wheatsheaf at the rear of Percy Street. It was here that the now famous Charles Forte had a depot for his milk delivery business in the late 1930s.

30. *Fitzroy Chapel*

PERCY STREET

A street of fine 18th century houses, some refaced and altered internally, but now overshadowed by both Metropolis House facing Tottenham Court Road and the EMI development. It still retains a good mixture of residential, shops and workshop space. A number of houses still retain the original plasterwork and finely carved doorcases while No 4 has been faced with very attractive Art Nouveau tiles. The name of the street may well be derived from the Percy coffee house which stood on the corner of Percy Street and Rathbone Place from 1768-1839.

No 1

Now called the White Tower and one of the most expensive restaurants in the area, it was originally a restaurant and hotel called the Tour Eiffel. It served for many years the more affluent writers and artists of Fitzrovia. In 1910 it was acquired by an Austrian, Rudolf Stulik, who remained patron throughout the 'golden age' of Fitzrovia. In 1914 the Vorticists, formed around Wyndham Lewis and Ezra Pound, met here to celebrate the launching of their magazine *'BLAST'*. The Vorticists attacked all that was dear to the artistic establishment and adopted many of the ideas of the Italian and European Futurist movement; members included Wadsworth, Helen Saunders and Jacob Epstein as well as Wyndham Lewis, after he broke away from Fry's Omega Studios. Wyndham Lewis and Helen Saunders painted the walls of one of Stulik's upper rooms and this is recorded in a painting of the Vorticists celebrating the launching of *BLAST* by William Roberts, also a member, now to be seen in the Tate Gallery. The wall painting was subsequently destroyed and no record of it now exists.

In the 1930s Augustus John and his circle and writers like Dylan Thomas could be found here. In 1943 the restaurant transferred to Greek ownership and took on its present name.

No 4

Percy Wyndham Lewis had rooms here in 1914 and is supposed to have spent much of his time in bed writing his first novel, *Tarr*. In the 1930s he was living at No 31.

No 5

Here lived William Franks from 1770-88. He played an important role in the development of Percy Street, Rathbone Street and Charlotte Street.

No 12

Henry Pierce Bone, a painter and son of the more famous artist Henry Bone lived here from 1832-46, then at No 22 where he died.

No 14

Coventry Patmore, poet and essayist spent about a year here in 1863. He gave support to the Pre-Raphaelite Brotherhood in their early days and contributed to their publication, *The Germ*.

No 23

William Cowper (1731-1800), the author and poet on English rural life from Olney in Buckinghamshire, stayed here with friends in 1792.

No 28

Vanessa Bell, the painter and co-founder of Omega Studios, shared a flat here with Duncan Grant from 1955 to her death in 1961. Much of their latter years were spent painting at their country house at Charleston, Sussex.

RATHBONE PLACE

Rathbone Place, which connects the lower end of Charlotte Street with Oxford Street, was one of the first streets to be developed in the area in about 1720. It was originally lined with houses of some quality but these were soon overtaken by commercial uses. A few of the original houses still stand at the north end but altered almost beyond recognition. The west side has almost completely disappeared to make way for the Post Office's W1 sorting office — an architectural disaster.

No 6

The Black Horse public house. A pub of this name stood here by 1746 when what is now Evelyn Yard ran off Rathbone Place and was called Black Horse Stable Yard. Today access to the yard can be gained from both Gresse Street and Rathbone Place, next to the pub.

No 12

William Hazlitt, the essayist and literary critic lived here from 1799 to 1803. In the Post Office directory for 1863 Henry Brinsmead, piano-maker and relative of John Brinsmead, had a shop or workshop here.

No 17

John Flaxman, the sculptor, lived here for a time before moving to 7 Greenwell Street, just off Cleveland Street. He was a frequent visitor to the house of the Rev. Henry Mathew, first minister of the Percy Chapel, at No 27.

No 25

The Wheatsheaf; one of a series of pubs owned by the brewers Youngers in central London, which was constructed between the wars in a mock Tudor style. It was a favourite haunt of writers and artists during the second war and it is said that Dylan Thomas was first introduced to his future wife, Caitlin McNamara, here in 1936 by Augustus John.

No 27

Here lived the Rev. Henry and Mrs Mathew, the vicar of the Percy Chapel from 1766-1804. Mathew was a patron of Flaxman in his early years who in return carved small figures in niches

31. The Wheatsheaf, Rathbone Place, 1981

in their back-room, then used as a library. Mrs Mathew was also a great patron of the arts and her regular 'conversaziones' allowed writers and poets to reach a wide and discerning audience. J. T. Smith, whose reminiscences of the area are recorded in his *Book for a Rainy Day*, once heard William Blake reading poetry here. Mrs Mathew later helped him publish a volume of early poems. She was also a great supporter of Italian composers of the time, before they had become widely accepted in this country.

No 33

John Harris Heal, founder of the family firm which continues today in Tottenham Court Road, set up his bed-making and furniture business here after starting as a feather dresser in Leicester Square. In 1808 he moved the business to 203 Tottenham Court Road.

Nos 38 and 39

Winsor and Newton, suppliers of artists' materials, opened one of their first shops here.

No 44

Nathaniel Hone R.A. (1718-1784), lived and died here. J. T. Smith in *Nollekens and His Times* reports a dispute this artist had with Sir Joshua Reynolds over characters portrayed in his painting, the *Conjuror*.

No 49

George Jackson & Sons made architectural ornaments here from about 1790 to the early 1930s. They were the first firm to use carton-pierre, a fibrous plaster suitable for mouldings and ornaments, which was first developed in France, and are said to have worked to the designs of Robert Adam in the early years.

Nos 51 and 52

George Rowney & Co., artists' colour manufacturers, have had a shop here for at least a century.

RATHBONE STREET

This has been variously known as Upper Rathbone Place, Glanville Street and Benet Street until its present name was adopted. A number of the original buildings have survived on the west side, including the Newman Arms and the Dickensian Newman Passage.

No 47

The Duke of York. An attractive building in its own right; also known as a meeting place for the beatniks soon after the war.

RICHARDSON MEWS

Like most of the mews in the area, originally built for stabling for nearby houses in Fitzroy Square and Warren Street. The origin of the name is unknown but probably relates to the name of a former user. Today, nothing survives of any note and the mews is awaiting redevelopment for housing.

SCALA STREET

Originally called Pitt Street after the 18th century prime minister, it was lined with modest but attractive houses. With the building of the Scala theatre *(see under Tottenham Street)* in the 1890s most of the north side was demolished. The south side remains largely intact and a number of these houses have recently been renovated by Camden Council to good effect.

STEPHEN MEWS

This runs off Gresse Street from the former Bricklayers' Arms, parallel to Stephen Street. Very few of the original buildings have survived.

It was here that the fringe German anarchist International Club met in the 1880s. The Club was connected to the Socialist League of which at one time both William Morris and Frank Kitz *(see 72 Grafton Way)* were members, but catered mainly for the European emigrés who lived in the area in considerable numbers. In May 1885 the police raided the Club, supported by an hysterical mob that stormed the place in the wake of the police and stripped it bare.

STEPHEN STREET

At one time a street of fine Georgian houses, linking Gresse Street with Tottenham Court Road, it was systematically emptied and demolished house by house in the early 1970s to prevent any opposition to the new EMI office development. Many long-standing tenants and small workshops were ousted in the process.

No 2

Pierre Langlois, a prestigious furniture maker and specialist in floral marquetry, had a workshop here. He executed many commissions for the nobility, including the Duke of Bedford and Horace Walpole. Langlois lived close by his workshop at 39 Tottenham Court Road in the 1760s and '70s and is one of the first furniture makers to move into the area soon after it was built. His beautifully engraved trade card is preserved in the Heal Collection and a commode built by him can be seen at the National Trust house called the Vyne in Hampshire.

TORRINGTON PLACE

Originally called Francis Street, this was developed by the Bedford Estate in the late 18th century. Today no original buildings survive and it is mainly known for its large blocks of mansion flats — Woburn Mansions on the corner with Huntley Street, Gordon Mansions on the north side and Ridgmount Gardens on the south. Pevsner ascribes Ridgmount Gardens to C. Fitzroy Doll, architect to the Bedford Estate, in what he describes as 'Franco-Flemish Gothic style', built in 1907. Gordon Mansions was built about the same time in a similar style and may well be by the same architect. Both blocks were built on gardens and a mews owned by the Bedford Estate.

TOTTENHAM COURT ROAD

Tottenham Court Road has always been one of London's major thoroughfares leading northwards to Hampstead, either from Westminster or from the City via High Holborn and St Giles High Street. When Whitefield's chapel was built in 1756, the street was still bordered on both sides by fields and hawthorn hedges, with only the southern-most part developed to any great extent. In the following 50 years development proceeded rapidly, first on the west side then on the east, so that by the turn of the century development had reached the New Road and continued up the Hampstead Road.

In the late 18th and early 19th centuries a considerable number of craftsmen and cabinet makers had established workshops here and by 1838 Tallis's elevations show a thriving street of shops and trades of all descriptions. From these early beginnings of craftsmen setting up workshops and perhaps later opening shops in the same building, by the late 19th century Tottenham Court Road had become London's leading shopping street for furniture, bedding and associated furnishings. It was also one of the first streets to be provided with electric lighting. Heal's, Maple's,

32. No 26 Tottenham Court Road, 1903

33. Nos 9/10 Tottenham Court Road, 1904

Shoolbred's, T. W. Thompson, Oetzmann and Catesby's are just some of the larger stores that flourished around the turn of the century. It is indeed fortunate that with the building of what is now the Northern line underground both sides of Tottenham Court Road were photographed building by building in 1908. These are preserved in the Swiss Cottage Library.

The numbering has not changed and proceeds from the west side at the south end up to Euston Road and then down the east side from north to south. This will be followed below.

No 6

The Blue Posts. A pub of the same name was recorded here in 1770, on the corner of Hanway Street, and in 1808 an hourly coach service ran from here to Hampstead.

No 19

A pub called the Black Horse stood on the corner with Tudor Place (now demolished to make way for the EMI development) at least from the 1740s. Tudor Place, formerly Black Horse Yard, was a circular court yard which at one time provided stabling for the pub. It survived as small workshops and warehouses until the early 1970s.

No 46

The Rising Sun. Externally one of the most

34. The Rising Sun, 46 Tottenham Court Road, 1981

35. The Rev. George Whitefield

unusual and attractive pubs in the area by Treadwell and Martin, 1897, which Pevsner describes as 'in a fanciful Art Nouveau Gothic'. A large section of Tottenham Court Road and parts of Percy Street and Windmill Street were 'lost' with the building of the totally inappropriate Metropolis House.

No 64

At the corner of Goodge Street once stood the Talbot, later replaced by Catesby's furniture store.

No 76

A bomb fell close by the Whitefield church and destroyed most of Nos 76 and 77. These were rebuilt to look almost exactly as they had before. In No 76 Alderman Donald McGregor, mayor of St Pancras 1906-7, lived.

THE WHITEFIELD MEMORIAL CHURCH

George Whitefield (1714-70), the famous evangelical preacher had been minister at the Long Acre Chapel when, due to his ability to pull large congregations, attracted opposition from the vicar of St Martins-in-the-Fields. He therefore sought ground on which to build up a chapel outside the built-up area. With the help of supporters like the Countess of Huntingdon he was able to raise the necessary capital to acquire a seven year lease from Francis and William Goodge from 1756 on a piece of land in the north east corner of Walnut Tree Field. This was close to a large pond called the Little Sea, probably formed from the extraction of brick clay. The chapel was designed by Matthew Pearce and the foundation stone was laid in 1756. It was opened to the public the same winter. The chapel was roughly square in plan with a hipped roof surmounted by a bell-cote. The eastern face had an applied façade of four pilasters carrying an entablature and pediment. The lease was renewed by the Fitzroy family until 1828 when the freehold of the site was put up for sale.

Whitefield preached here to large congregations and by 1759 an extension was needed on the east side of the chapel. He then spent some years in the USA where he died in 1770. John Wesley preached at a memorial service for Whitefield in the chapel on 30th November 1770.

In 1827 the chapel with adjoining almshouses and the minister's house was put up for sale but was withdrawn and shortly afterwards the freehold was acquired by the Trustees. The chapel was thereupon renovated and reopened for services in 1831. In February 1857 the whole building was destroyed by fire and the site was acquired by the London Congregational Building Society, which constructed a new chapel designed by John Tarring. Owing to subsidence, probably resulting from the Little Sea, the chapel became unsafe and was closed in 1889. A new building was finally completed a decade later, only to be destroyed by a flying bomb in 1945. The present building reconstructed in the 1950s is used by the American community in London.

Among the burials recorded in the chapel are: Mrs Elizabeth Whitefield (d.1768), John Bacon, sculptor (d.1799), Matthew Pearce, architect of the first chapel (d.1775) and the Rev. Augustus Toplady, author of the hymn *Rock of Ages* (d.1778).

THE BURIAL GROUND

The survival of Whitfield Gardens today, just one part of the original burial ground, has resulted more from local determination than the beneficence of the church. Although the exact boundaries of the original piece of land acquired by Whitefield are uncertain, it is clear that from an early date the burial ground became an embarrassment and the chapel made several attempts to sell it off. 8-12 Tottenham Street, which were built as residences in the 19th century, were probably never part of the chapel lands but Georgian buildings certainly stood on the corner of Tottenham Street and Tottenham Court Road until they were bombed in 1945.

For at least a century the grounds were used regularly for burials, so much so that the land soon became a health risk as coffins were piled up one on top of the other. In 1798 a group of body-snatchers were intercepted by an observant watchman but others proved more successful, and the area soon became associated with the 'resurrection men'.

In order to remove the nuisance once and for all the chapel authorities made repeated attempts to sell the land for building. In 1865 an alliance between the relatives of the dead and local people resulted in an injunction being served to prevent developers preparing the ground for building. In response, the builders brought in 60 navvies to smash up the tombs, amidst what one contemporary report called 'the yells, groans, and execrations of the populace, who assembled outside the ground despite the nauseous effluvia caused by the digging'.

After further attempts to develop the land in 1873 the local MP, Sir Julian Goldsmid, stepped in and offered to lay out the park at his own expense. The Vestry also attempted to purchase the land to no avail and after years of litigation the LCC eventually obtained the necessary powers in 1895 to provide and maintain it as a public park. In the 1880s a festival of sorts took place here and apart from the usual side-shows, 'a brass band played the accompaniment to the trippers who did the light fantastic on the memorials to the dead'.

At the height of the blitz in 1940 eight deep shelters were authorised on the Northern line and two on the Central. The entrance to one of these was constructed in the burial ground just to the north of Whitfield church. Another entrance to this was in North Crescent; both are still visible. Each was designed to hold 8000 people although the one at Goodge Street was later allocated to the American Army and in 1942 part of it was adapted for use as Eisenhower's headquarters. After the war it remained as a military transit camp until May 1956 and was finally leased off in 1974 for the storage of books by the British Library.

No 130

The former Grafton Nurses' Home which was requisitioned soon after the war for medical use. Prior to that it had been the Grafton Hotel. Her biographer records that Lady Ottoline Morrell, the half sister of the Duke of Portland and Bloomsbury socialite, spent two nights here with Bertrand Russell during their brief affair in 1911.

36. *Maple's furniture store, 1935*

Nos 141-150

This stark development by Seifert which now houses Maple's and the Housing Corporation above, replaced the former Maple's building — one of the most serious architectural losses the area has suffered since the war.

Nos 151-162

The former site of Shoolbred's store, now replaced by an undeveloped car park and the Empire Rooms and Paramount Court. James Shoolbred first opened a draper's shop in Broad Street, Bloomsbury about 1820 and in order to

37. Heal's old store

expand the business moved to Tottenham House at 155 Tottenham Court Road. James Shoolbred died in 1862 and his two sons gradually acquired adjoining properties until the store occupied the whole of the block, including part of Grafton Way East.

Nos 163-168

The site of T. W. Thompson's drapers' store, which extended down as far as the entrance to Mortimer Market. This site has now been redeveloped for offices although the entrance to Mortimer Market survives.

No 183

The New Inn; a pub with the same name stood here in the 18th century and was known for the pits at the back where dog fights were held.

No 191

Until 1961 a building stood here on the corner of Torrington Place which had previously been a pub called Apollo and the Muses. It was an exotic creation by C. Fitzroy Doll, architect to the Bedford Estate and a St Pancras councillor, built in 1898. The front was decorated by life-size terracotta statues of Apollo and the muses made by Doulton at Lambeth. One of these was presented to the mayor of St Pancras and now stands in St George's Gardens, Camden.

Nos 191-199

Heal's store. It was John Harris Heal's widow, Fanny, who took over the firm on his death and acquired first No 196 and the adjoining properties later. In 1907 Ambrose Heal became chairman and in 1917 instructed architects Smith and Brewer to build the present shop, necessitating the demolition of the old farmhouse behind. In 1961-2 the shop was extended sympathetically by

Fitzroy Robinson & Partners on the Tottenham Court Road frontage and down Torrington Place. Heal's always prided themselves in fostering the best in the design of furnishings and fabrics, especially where this involved British craftsmen. The fact that they are the only surviving large store of this kind in Tottenham Court Road is perhaps a tribute to this policy.

In the early part of the century, Heal's Mansard Gallery was used for exhibitions of avant garde art. In 1913 an exhibition was held of works by artists such as Roger Fry, Duncan Grant and Mark Gertler.

Ambrose Heal's collection, which he donated to the St Pancras library, is now an invaluable source of material for local historians in Camden.

Nos 263-279

On the site of the Horseshoe public house (formerly a hotel) and the Dominion cinema once stood the famous Meux brewery. Meux began brewing here in 1764 but before then an earlier brewery had been run by John Hassell, who in 1717 took a lease on part of Crab Tree Field and lived in a large house in the Gresse Street area. In 1814 an explosion of two vats created a near riot when vast quantities of liquor ran down the street. In 1816 the brewery was stormed by rioters protesting against the Tory ministry and particularly the Lords Liverpool and Sidmouth.

The Horseshoe Hotel was designed by Finch Hill and E. L. Paraire for publican Charles Best in 1875. At the time it was an ambitious development, combining a pub, restaurant, grill, cafe and hotel. In 1890 it was acquired by the Baker brothers who also built the Tottenham public house just round the corner in Oxford Street.

TOTTENHAM MEWS

A mews off Tottenham Street with a number of warehouses and light industrial buildings still intact on the east side. On the west side buildings were occupied by a gun-maker and brass foundry in the late 19th century.

TOTTENHAM STREET

Fitzrovia, along with the Curtain Road area of the East End, was the centre of furniture making in the 19th century. Henry Mayhew, in *London Labour and the London Poor*, contrasts the wages and living conditions of those craftsmen who were members of trade societies and those subject to free market forces. One such society he visited was the Woodcarvers' Society, which he describes as:

'On the first floor of a small private house in Tottenham Street, Tottenham Court Road, is, so to speak, the museum of the working men belonging to this branch of the cabinet-makers. The walls of the back room are hung around with plaster casts of some of the choicest specimens of the arts, and in the front room the table is strewn with volumes of valuable prints and drawings in connexion with the craft. Round this table are ranged the members of the society — some forty or fifty were there on the night of my attendance — discussing the affairs of the trade.'

No 15

The Hope; in 1839 this was Ginn's coffee house.

Nos 21-25

The Scala theatre was redeveloped in the early 1970s and although a cinema survives in the basement, the office and residential building above ground floor level is little more than a monument to the developer's greed. The Scala was only the last name for a number of theatrical enterprises, most of which seem to have been doomed to failure.

The first building on the site facing Tottenham Street was a concert room built by Francis Pasquali in 1772, which proved so successful that in 1780 it was enlarged and refitted by James Wyatt and was often visited by George III and Queen Charlotte. In 1802 the building became known as the Cognoscenti theatre and was used by a private theatrical club known as the Pic-Nics. In 1808 the rooms were briefly used as a circus but by 1810 it had reverted back to a theatre. It was extended on the Scala Street side and a portico was added over the Tottenham Street entrance. This opened in 1810 as the Tottenham theatre with a production of *Love in a Village*. This proved a spectacular failure and in 1815 the theatre was again altered and reopened as the Regency theatre.

After a further series of failures and changes in name — the Queen's, the Fitzroy and the Prince of Wales were all tried at different times — the theatre closed in 1882 and remained vacant until it was bought by the Salvation Army as a hostel in 1886. In 1902 a surgeon, Distin Maddick, purchased the theatre and adjoining property in Charlotte Street and opened a new and enlarged theatre called the Scala in 1904, to a design of Frank T. Verity. This proved as unsuccessful as previous ventures and in 1911 it was taken over as one of the earliest cinemas, showing *Birth of a Nation*, for example, in 1915.

During the 1930s the theatre was used for productions of Ralph Reader's *Gang Show* and during the war theatrical performances had a brief revival. In 1943 it became the temporary home of the US Army Theatre Unit. Amateur performances continued, interspersed with Christmas pantomimes such as *Peter Pan*, until 1969, and since the fabric of the building was rapidly deteriorating there was little enthusiasm for maintaining a theatre on the site. In 1972 planning permission was granted for redevelopment, with the stipulation that a building for public assembly should be included on the site. Initially the Other Cinema occupied the basement — later becoming the Scala cinema — but this was forced to close in May 1981 to make way for the Fourth Television Channel company.

No 26
In 1839 this was the Middlesex coffee house.

No 42
In 1828 Richard Parkes Bonington, the landscape painter, a number of whose works now hang in the Wallace Collection, was brought here to die. The house was then occupied by John Dixon, an engraver.

No 49
In the basement the Communist Working Men's Club met between 1878-1902. This was one of the many radical political organisations that were supported by expatriate European socialists who lived and worked in the area. Marx, Engels and William Morris were either members or frequent visitors. In 1902 the club moved to 107 Charlotte Street.

The easternmost part of the street was originally called Chapel Street and here lived the landscape painter, Richard Wilson (1714-83) in his last years. In 1771 he lived at 78 Charlotte Street (c.f.)

UNIVERSITY STREET
This runs from Tottenham Court Road to Gower Street, immediately opposite the entrance to University College. On part of the north side is University College Hospital, which was built in 1897-1906 and was designed by Alfred Waterhouse. Construction cost £250,000 which was donated by Sir John Blundell Maple, the store-owner and MP for Dulwich.

No 22
Here lived John T. Smith (1766-1833), who in 1816 was made Keeper of Prints at the British Museum. His two books, '*A Book for a Rainy Day*' and '*Nollekens and his Times*', provide a wealth of information and anecdote about Fitzrovia in the late 18th century. In the first he claimed to have been born in a hackney cab on the way to his parents' house at 38 Great Portland Street and many of his reminiscences are based on stories told to him by his father, who was an assistant to Nollekens, the sculptor, then living in Mortimer Street.

WARREN MEWS
A narrow mews off Warren Street, the east side of which is occupied by the workshops of Louis Koch Ltd. (*see 106 Cleveland Street*). They claim this building was previously used by Maple's for the stabling of sick horses, which were used for their delivery vehicles.

WARREN STREET
A street probably built by a number of different speculative builders in the 1790s because each house differs in substantial details, but which together create a fine Georgian set-piece. Their present deplorable condition is a reflection of

38. Derelict property, 63 Warren Street, 1981

39. Dr. William Kitchiner

50 years of blight created by the presence of used car dealers occupying the ground floors. Two large property companies also own sections of the street and they seem to be waiting for the elements to complete a slow demolition job. Like surrounding streets, Warren Street was colonised early on by artists and particularly engravers.

No 10
Here lived Abraham Raimbach from 1808-38. He is best known for engraving Wilkie's pictures, such as the *Village Politicians*.

No 43
Dr William Kitchiner, the eccentric doctor, gourmet and writer on medical and scientific subjects, lived here until his death in 1827.

No 56
Charles Turner, the mezzotint engraver, lived here from 1799-1803. He then moved to No 50 from 1803 to his death in 1857.

No 63
James Mitan (1776-1823), the engraver, lived here from 1808-1823. He married Charlotte, daughter of William Gowing, the builder who played a large part in the development of the Charlotte Street area.

No 65
Public opinion was outraged, or at least so the press claimed at the time, when it was revealed in the divorce court that Sir Charles Dilke (1843-1911), a leading Liberal politician, had had an affair with Mrs Crawford, the wife of a Home Office official. In court it was claimed the couple met secretly in the first floor back room of this house, which was rented by a former servant of Dilke. As a result of the publicity attached to the case in July 1886, Dilke was forced to resign both as MP for Chelsea and President of the Local Government Board.

40. St Pancras Baths and Washhouses c1877 in Whitfield Street

No 68

R. W. Buss, the painter best known for his theatrical portraits, lived in this house.

No 73

Another court case which received considerable public attention, this time a double murder is associated with this house. In December 1854 Mr Moore, a soda water manufacturer who lived at this address, was murdered after Emanuel Barthelemy had called at the door. The murderer ran out into Euston Road where he also shot Mr Collard, a former police officer turned greengrocer who happened to live at 74 Warren Street, while trying to apprehend him. A crowd which was attracted by the incident then marched Barthelemy off to the police station. While the murderer was hung at the Old Bailey, a subscription fund was opened to provide a grave for Collard's body in the St Pancras cemetery in Finchley.

WHITFIELD PLACE

This is an interesting space at the north end of Whitfield Street which has survived intact, despite undergoing several changes of use. It was laid out in the late 18th century as the Fitzroy Market with open stalls in the centre and surrounded by small shops.

In the mid 19th century the site was occupied by the St John the Evangelist boys school, attached to the St John the Evangelist church in Charlotte Street. In 1876 the site was acquired by the St Pancras Vestry from the London School Board and a year later the building of the St Pancras baths was begun, designed by Horace Gundry in a Moorish style. The baths were bombed in the war and the site remained a temporary car park until in 1977 the Fitzrovia Play Association launched a fund-raising campaign to provide a playspace and sitting area. This was opened by local MP Frank Dobson in 1979.

WHITFIELD STREET

Named after George Whitefield, the spelling unaccountably changed. It was originally known as John Street from Windmill Street to Howland Street, Upper John Street from Howland Street to Maple Street and Hertford Street northwards to Warren Street. Since the street runs north-south it was developed in a piecemeal fashion and never

41. An early Indian restaurant in the area — 1945 at 137 Whitfield Street

achieved the social eminence or commercial success of, say, Charlotte Street. The northern section was completed around 1800 with a single terrace of houses and was noted for a series of well preserved early 19th century shopfronts. A number of these buildings have been demolished or collapsed in recent years, although plans do exist to reconstruct the terrace for residential use. The remainder of the street has almost totally been replaced by new buildings.

Nos 6-18

Until the Second World War the St John the Evangelist National schools were on this site.

Nos 17-25

The site of these buildings, formerly an attractive row of shops, has been a car park since 1944 when the area was bombed. They were built on the site of a brewery slightly later than the rest of the street. Part of Colville Place was destroyed by the same bomb. Fortunately an engraving of these buildings survives.

No 36

On the site of what is now the service access to Tesco's once stood an institution which played an important part in the political life of the capital; the Scientific and Literary Institute. From its foundation in 1840 by followers of Robert Owen to its closure in 1858, it provided a regular meeting place for a number of secular and political organisations, all of which contributed to the development of radical politics in London. Most notable were co-operative organisations based on the ideas of Robert Owen, who built the working community of New Lanark in Scotland. The National Secular Society, the Chartists and emergent trades unions like the West End Shoemakers also held regular meetings here. On 10th April 1848 a large crowd of Chartists were addressed here by Fergus O'Connor, then MP for

42. Scientific and Literary Institute, Whitfield Street

Nottingham and a Chartist leader, before the famous march to Parliament from Kennington Common.

No 41 (and 1 Scala Street)

Pollock's Toy Museum combines both a unique museum of mainly 19th century toys, dolls and dolls' houses from all over the world and a shop selling toy theatres, prints and reproductions of 19th century toys. The toy theatre business was founded by John Redington, a compositor, in 1851 at 208 Hoxton Old Town. In his spare time he printed miniatures of scripts, characters, scenery and the proscenium arches from the London theatre of the period 1811-30 for sale in his shop. On his death in 1872 the business was taken over by his daughter Eliza who in 1873 married a furrier, Ben Pollock. They kept the business going until 1895 when Eliza died and her place was taken by Louise, the eldest daughter. In 1936 Ben Pollock died but Louise and her sister kept the shop going, then renamed as 73 Hoxton Street, until it was bombed in the war when they decided to sell out. In 1955 Marguerite Fawdry bought up the stock of the company and set up shop in an attic at 44 Monmouth Street, WC2. It was then decided to start the museum, based mainly on personal gifts and loans in order to attract more customers. In 1969 more space was needed so the whole enterprise moved to 1 Scala Street and later the adjoining house at 41 Whitfield Street was taken on to house both the shop and museum. Today the Fawdrys run Pollocks as an educational trust and are visited by hundreds of foreign tourists and school parties every year.

Nos 54-60

This building was purpose-built for one or more companies of goldbeaters; symbols of the trade can still be seen on the front façade. In 1863 at least one goldbeater is recorded as occupying premises in this part of Whitfield Street and in 1938 three goldbeaters and one manufacturer of gold leaf used this building.

No 108

Dr Marie Stopes (1880-1958) was born in Edinburgh but her parents moved to London soon after her birth. She read a science degree at University College London, later transferring to Munich University, where her interest in birth

43. The young Dr Marie Stopes, photo by Maull and Fox

control first developed. After her first unsuccessful marriage she wrote her first book, *Married Love*, and in 1918 married Humphrey Roe, who remained a keen supporter of her work. Together they opened the first clinic of its kind in March 1921 at Marlborough Road, Holloway, then as now a depressed area of Islington. In 1925 they decided to move to this address where the 'Mothers' Clinic for Constructive Birth Control' was opened. Despite war damage the clinic remained open and continues today as the Well Women Centre.

WINDMILL STREET

One of the earliest streets to be developed in the area although for many years previously it had been a farm track leading from Tottenham Court Road to the windmill in Charlotte Street. Building leases were granted on the south side by John Goodge in 1723-4 but most of the houses were not completed until 1760-70. Many of the houses have been altered subsequently, particularly on the ground floors, but its original character as a quiet residential street can still be imagined without too much difficulty.

No 6

After a split in the Socialist League a group of anarchists formed the Club Autonomie, which in February 1886 met at 32 Charlotte Street, then moved to this address. For some time the north London branch of the Socialist League held meetings here. However, the club eventually became almost impossible to use because of the continual presence of police spies and after the Greenwich Park bombing in 1894 the club was one of the first places to be raided by the police.

John Quail's book, *The Slow Burning Fuse*, gives an interesting insight into the world of 19th century anarchism. A contemporary report of the Greenwich Park bombing suggests there were 'some 7000 to 8000 Anarchists, of whom 2000 were Russian Jews in the East End, 1000 were Germans living mainly around Soho Square and the Middlesex Hospital plus a small and violent colony of 400 French Anarchists living in the Charlotte Street area'.

44. *No 231 Tottenham Court Road, 1903*

No 12

In 1776 the St Pancras Female Charity School was founded here, originally taking six young girls but later increasing to about 40. In 1790 the school moved to a site in the Hampstead Road given by the Southampton Estate. The annual report for 1791, a copy of which is in the Heal Collection, lists Lady Southampton as the patroness and Samuel Foyster as treasurer. Foyster was at the time a local landowner since in 1778 he inherited lands belonging to William Goodge, his uncle. The report also records that the trustees of the school had agreed that girls reaching a certain age were being 'put out to service' with approved families. In 1904 the school was rebuilt on the same site and when it later moved to West Hill, Highgate, this became the nurses' home next to the National Temperance Hospital.

No 13

It is possible that the Middlesex Hospital was at this address when it opened on the south side of the street in 1745. In 1756 it moved to its present location in Mortimer Street on land acquired from Lord Berners.

No 17

William Jupp the Younger lived here. He was architect and surveyor to the Skinners', Merchant Taylors', Ironmongers' and Apothecaries' Companies and in 1808 designed the façade of the Skinners' Hall, Dowgate Hill in the City, which still survives. In 1831 he was made Master of the Carpenters' Company.

In the 19th century this house became a pub called the White Hart, which in the 1920s was kept by Daisy Dormer, the music hall artiste, and her husband Albert Gee. He used to perform in a music hall act called the Brothers Egbert. It was an old fashioned pub with photos of actors and actresses on the walls, a green parrot in a cage and as often as not, somebody playing the banjo or piano. This part of the street was bombed during the war and in the 1960s a pub with the same name was incorporated into a larger development.

No 36

Henry Morland, portrait painter and father of George Morland the landscape painter lived here in 1779. In 1797 he died while living in Stephen Street.

45. *The Fitzroy Tavern, 1981*

No 43

The Fitzroy Tavern stands on the corner of Windmill Street and Charlotte Street. The present building was constructed in 1897 and was designed by W. M. Brutton, a prolific pub architect, although a coffee house occupied the house at least as early as 1833. In the 1920s and '30s the Fitzroy was a meeting place for artists in the area — particularly the circle round Augustus John — and in the 1940s people like Dylan Thomas, Julian Maclaren-Ross, Nina Hamnett, George Orwell and Alan Ross drank their way through the war years. In this 'Golden Age' it was also frequented by artists of a literary bent like John Lehmann, Cyril Connolly and the poet and editor Tambimuttu. It was not long before the place became choked with service men and hangers-on and many moved to the more secluded pubs like the Wheatsheaf or Marquis of Granby.

It was the editor of *Poetry (London)*, J. M. Tambimuttu who issued the following warning to a young writer, Julian Maclaren-Ross, during a night of heavy drinking:

'Only beware of Fitzrovia,' Tambi said ...... 'It's a dangerous place, you must be careful.'

'Fights with knives?'

'No, a worse danger. You might get Sohoitis you know.'

'No I don't. What is it?'

'If you get Sohoitis', Tambi said very seriously, 'you will stay there always day and night and get no work done ever. You have been warned.'

Further Reading

Volume XXI of the *Survey of London* is an excellent starting point for a detailed description of the development of the area, its buildings and a brief mention of some of the many famous residents who have lived here over the past two hundred years. Beresford Chancellor's *'London's Old Latin Quarter'* — now out of print — is the only history of the area, but was written about a decade before 'Fitzrovia' came into common usage. The two books by J. T. Smith are collections of stories and anecdotes about the area and its inhabitants, mainly told to him by his father who was an assistant to Nollekens, the sculptor who lived in Mortimer Street. The Ambrose Heal collection in Camden's Swiss Cottage library is a vast store of original material without which this study would have been almost impossible. There are many other novels and biographies which are set in the area or give a feeling of what it was like to live here at different times, which were drawn on but which are too numerous to list below:

G. Bebbington. *London Street Names*. Batsford, 1972.

E. Beresford Chancellor. *London's Old Latin Quarter*. Jonathan Cape, 1930.

George Clinch. *Marylebone and St. Pancras*. Truslove and Shirley, 1890.

Bernard Falk. *The Royal Fitz Roys*. Hutchinson, 1950.

Constantine Fitzgibbon. *The Life of Dylan Thomas*. J. Dent, 1965.

W. Godfrey and W. Marcham. *Tottenham Court Road and Neighbourhood. (The Parish of St. Pancras, Part III). The Survey of London Vol. XXI*. LCC, 1949.

Ambrose Heal. *The London Furniture Makers*. Dove Publications, 1972.

Peter Hall. *The Industries of London*. Hutchinson, 1962.

Robert Hewison. *Under Siege: Literary Life in London 1939-45*. Weidenfeld and Nicholson, 1977.

Stephen Knight. *Jack the Ripper: The Final Solution*. Harrap, 1976.

John Quail. *The Slow Burning Fuse: The Lost History of British Anarchists*. Paladin, 1978.

Richard Shone. *Bloomsbury Portraits: Vanessa Bell, Duncan Grant and their Circle*. Phaidon, 1976.

John T. Smith. *Nollekens and his Times*. (first published in two volumes, 1828). Turnstile Press, 1949.

John T. Smith. *A Book for a Rainy Day*. Methuen, 1905.

Gladys Scott Thompson. *The Russells in Bloomsbury*. Cape, 1940.

G. G. Williams. *A Guide to Literary London*. Batsford, 1973.

Index